SERVANT LEADERSHIP BOOTCAMP:

Twelve Knockout Steps to Develop Mental Strength
through Empathy and GRIT

CARA BRAMLETT, PA-C

Servant Leadership Bootcamp: Twelve Knockout Steps to Develop Mental Strength through Empathy and GRIT

© 2019 Cara Bramlett

Leadership Development Series, Book 3

Disclaimer and FTC Notice

This book is for entertainment purposes only. The views expressed are those of the author alone and should not be taken as expert instruction or commands. It is read with the understanding that the publisher and author are not engaged to render any type of psychological, legal, or any other kind of professional advice. The reader is responsible for his or her own actions.

Adherence to all applicable laws and regulations including international, federal, state, and local governing professional licensing, business practices, advertising, and all other aspects of doing business in the US, Canada, or any other jurisdiction is the sole responsibility of the purchaser or reader.

While all attempts have been made to verify the information provided in this publication, neither the author nor the publisher assumes any responsibility for errors, omissions, or contrary interpretations of the subject matter herein. Also, neither the author nor the publisher assumes any responsibility or liability whatsoever on the behalf of the purchaser or reader of these materials.

Any perceived slight of any individual or organization is purely unintentional.

I may use affiliate links and affiliate products I have used and found useful in the contents. If you decide to make a purchase, I will get a sales commission. This does not reflect that my opinion is for sale. I encourage you to do your own research before making any purchase online.

Mentor:

Gundi Gabrielle
Amazon Top 100 Authors
http://sassyzengirl.com
https://claimyourfreedomnow.com

Editor:

Nancee-Laetitia Marin
The Language Agent
http://thelanguageagent.com

Cover Designer:

Vanessa Mendozzi
Reedsy
https://reedsy.com

Dedicated to my husband,

Michael A. Bramlett,

for helping me discover my mental strength.

Table of Contents

Grit: It's What's for Breakfast

Some exceed because they are
destined, but most exceed because
of determination.

Anonymous

If you are reading this page, you are feeling the need to up your mental strength and grit. Perhaps you have been told you are a weak leader, emotional, or wear your heart on your sleeve. Perhaps you find yourself questioning your decisions, your skills, and your ability to lead. Considering quitting with the leadership-is-not-for-me mentality?

Ever doubt yourself? Ever think, I do not have the skills to lead such a big group? Maybe feel like you cannot even lead your household at times. Do you emotionally beat yourself up if things do not go exactly as planned?

Everyone in some way is a leader. Every day you lead up, across, and down. Leading down is the most common as you provide your team direction or manage your family. Leading across is by influence. You may not tell your partner or other managers what to do. However, you provide a compelling case as to why your way is the most valid. Leading up is also through influence. It is seen by providing or influencing more senior individuals by your actions.

You hold the cards and have the power.

You, the new manager with no formal training.

You, the one who leads by influence.

You, the leader who led for years and now are questioning your decisions.

You, the mom juggling kids, spouse, and work, wanting more from your career.

And you, the one who decided to take a chance in building grit.

Do you long to lead meetings where colleagues put down their phones, stop emailing, and listen while hanging onto your words?

Have you ever thought, I'll fake it till I make it? All the while, you feel like a fraud in your position.

You are not alone in these feelings. Right now, thousands of leaders are in your shoes. At some point along each leader's journey, one questions the ability to lead. The internal struggle shows through doubting skills, agitation, or frustration. Let's recognize it and call the struggle what it is—the imposter syndrome.

Did you know that 70 percent of leaders experience the imposter syndrome? Let's break that down. Think of the ten top leaders you respect and model after. Only three of them have lived their professional careers *not* feeling as a fraud.

Wow! Let that sink in for a moment!

Seventy percent felt they were imposters in their positions!

See, you are in good company!

I am no different.

At 30 years old, my father was diagnosed with metastatic colon cancer. Within two weeks of the diagnosis, he was hospitalized and passed away due to surgical complications of a bowel obstruction.

During the two weeks in intensive care, my father was on a ventilator and had multiple clots due to the increased clotting state induced by the cancer. One of the clots resulted in arm amputation. I made the hard medical decisions including removal of the ventilator. I questioned my decisions daily. I felt like a fraud in the hospital world. After all, I practiced clinic-based primary care.

One month later, I ended my marriage. I had been in a loveless relationship for over ten years. I was a fraud. Growing up, my life was filled with thoughts of finding my Prince Charming and having a lifetime marriage to one individual. It a difficult decision. One of the biggest challenges was my constant thoughts of failure and how I would be perceived by others.

I hit rock bottom. My life was moving fast and out of control. I turned to the only stable part of my life. I found comfort in my job. I love being a physician assistant and

11

treating patients. It is one of the places I seek joy.

Then the unthinkable happened. My employer brought me and five other NPs and PAs into a conference room. They told us what an amazing job we have done. We had changed the lives of the patients we served. Then they blankly shared that the contract had been terminated and our services were no longer required.

We were stunned and utterly confused.

What does this mean? Did we just get fired?

Yes, we did.

My next six months were the most painful of my life. My nights were often spent in monotonous routine. My dinner was consistently a glass of white wine and an Ativan, a common anxiety pill. I was severely depressed and begin having anxiety attacks. During the day, I put on a brave face and treated patient after patient. Night after night, I put my girls to bed and pulled the covers over my head to drown out my thoughts. I felt weak physically, emotionally, and mentally.

One day in my emotional stupor and sobbing cries, my sister told me to snap out of it because it was affecting Hannah, my oldest child. Hannah was only three years old. My sister was right, and it was exactly what I needed to hear.

I took a deep breath and pulled myself up by my bootstraps. I reached inside myself and found my mental strength to push through the trifecta of personal disasters.

I found myself. I found my voice again. I slowly put one

12

foot in front of the other and got my life in order. My wine-and-Ativan dinners were soon replaced with lean proteins and vegetables.

One year later, I was back to being a true mommy to my two little girls, got a better job in an on-site clinic, and found a new relationship with an incredible man.

Fast forward to today. I am an industry leader, lead a high-performing team of over a hundred individuals with a turnover rate of less than 5 percent. My imposter syndrome has been dormant for quite some while.

How did I get here? How did I rise again?

I had grit for breakfast.

Grit is the "perseverance and passion for long-term goals" (Duckworth, Peterson, Matthews, & Kelly, 2007). It is the passion that sustains long after motivation fails. The passion provides focus and will power to dig deep when nothing is left to give.

Know you are not alone on this journey of personal trials and leadership challenges. Each of us face obstacles every day. GRIT will lead you through hardships. The principles of servant leadership provide modeling for the best response to these hardships.

Imagine standing taller and demonstrating self-confidence in all your decisions. You have the ability to crush self-doubt, control your emotions, and create a culture of a thriving high-performing team.

You can do this! It is within your reach!

Let's start by checking your mental strength. Take the quick mental strength assessment at servantleaderjourney.com.

As a servant-leader, you create an environment of growth and development—the perfect environment to foster the development of grit. It's a place where your leadership welcomes challenges as opportunities, picks up adversity by bootstraps, and thrives to the next achievement.

This is the foundation of servant leadership. Grit cultivates the desire to lead and serve those led.

Grit is about perseverance of the things you are most passionate about. It is the mojo that keeps you going in times of difficulty and struggle. Grit is the secret success of your servant leadership journey.

Angela Duckworth, a psychologist at University of Pennsylvania, is a pioneer in the research of grit (Guts, Resilience, Initiative, Tenacity). Duckworth defines grit as "perseverance and passion for long-term goals." It is the essence or mojo that keeps individuals going until they achieve success.

An individual's leadership style is developed through your personal journey. It is a cultivation of personal experiences, leadership challenges, and mindset. Development thrives through one's response to each of these opportunities and lessons learned. Know that people are human—not perfect or indestructible. The process of healing and extending open hands to mend brokenness is a powerful transformation for the individual as well as the leader. It allows the leader to gain trust of the led—an honor and privilege not taken lightly and to be cherished as a precious gift.

This bootcamp is about the twelve knockout steps to discover and develop mental strength through leadership. Each step will be filled with self-discovery, understanding of your stumbling blocks, and your unique mindset. Each day you will develop strategies of busting through the mental obstacles that are holding you back and the tools to push you to the next level of achievement.

Let's start by checking your mental strength. Take the quick mental strength assessment at servantleaderjourney.com. Your score will guide you to the steps that will help you most in your journey.

No one leads like you. No one has your style or influence. You are an expression of your own experiences, trials, and victories. Throughout this journey, be honest with yourself and have an open growth mindset. Change and develop what is needed. There is no *right* way. There is only your way.

To lead you along the journey, you can download the GRIT Bootcamp Workbook. It is full of mental strength exercises to foster mental stamina you desire.

Throughout your journey, I am committed to you. I will believe in you when you have lost faith. I commit to help remind you of your aspirations to lead and serve the individuals you lead.

My goal is to help you achieve your potential and help you be stronger than yesterday!

Put on your gloves and let's get started!

Step 1:

What versus Why

Step 1: What versus Why

Purpose is the reason you journey. Passion is the fire that lights the way.

Anonymous

Every day men and women put themselves on the front line representing our country. They leave their families for months or years on end to serve others. Many barely make $30,000 per year, though risking life and limb.

Firefighters band together in brotherhood with waxed handlebar mustaches and iconic badge-of-honor tattoos that they wear proudly.

Police officers are the same. They are willing to lay their life on the line daily for their partners without concern for their personal safety—each vowing, I've got your back.

Why?

Why would someone purposefully seek out opportunities that could induce physical harm or possibly death?

Why would individuals take time away from their

families, miss childhood firsts that can never be brought back, or selflessly devote their life to a cause?

It's all about passion and purpose.

Step 1 is understanding that passion is the *what* and purpose is the *why*. Passion is the emotional drive of your biggest dream. It is the joy and love you have toward something. Passion generates the overwhelming and compelling emotions that lights a fire deep within you. Purpose is the why or deep reason of what you do. Purpose is your moral compass guiding actions to your passion. Purpose becomes the driving force and holistically completes you.

Passion is the drive to serve the greater good. The feeling of personal satisfaction in making a difference. The feeling that the world in some small way is a little better from your personal contributions. Passionate leaders focus on what is right and working well. Leaders without passion focus on things that are failing and off target.

There are several things that happen when a leader has passion:

- **Passion creates energy**. Passion generates energy to propel leaders forward. It becomes the inner strength that produces the fiery fuel. The passionate energy helps deal with difficult situations and obstacles.

- **Passion unveils vision**. Passion generates the fuel to produce the vision. The vision is frequently and passionately conveyed to the team in a way that others can see it, feel it, and envision the future.

- **Passion motivates others**. Passionate leaders are contagious to others. Being exposed to the passion inspires individuals to achieve greatness. The optimism and purpose retain employees to feel connected to something meaningful.

- **Passion leads by influence**. Passionate leaders have an authentic belief in the vision they are trying to achieve. People want to be part of something greater than themselves and are influenced to support the passion. It provides a meaning and purpose to daily tasks.

- **Passion generates potential**. Passionate leaders open doors to success for themselves as well as others. The continuous awareness to passion drives individuals out of their comfort zones and showcases their potential. The potential shown lessens the fear, propelling individuals to the next level.

- **Passion invites trust**. Passionate leaders naturally generate a sense of trust. Others recognize the passion as the leader's core value system. Then others believe the leader is doing what is in the best interest of the team or organization to meet the mission. The passionate leader's deep commitment, knowledge, and enthusiasm is conveyed.

Passionate leaders build on the present and prepare for

the future. They look at ways to evolve while keeping their passion in the forefront. They inspire as they move individuals toward change. Passionate leaders help others by cultivating each individual's passion and internal drive.

People are naturally attracted to passionate leaders. Many are searching for a higher purpose and ability to contribute to the greater good. Leaders draw them in and influences through conveying their vision. They lead others toward new ideas and change. Then the led becomes emotionally vested and connected to the passion.

Leadership is hard. There, I said it. I'll be the first to admit it. It is a completely different skill set and mentality. It is completely exhausting and overwhelming. Yet leadership is also the most exhilarating and self-satisfying experience.

Leadership is my passion. Supporting leaders when they have lost their mojo and the ones new to the craft is my purpose. Someone took a chance and believed in me. A huge chance! I was young, inexperienced, and would have a big team. My mentor believed in me when no one else did.

My inexperience led to mistakes and misjudgments. Peers declared that I was not cut out for this role: clinical people should stay in the clinic and not manage.

In these times of discouragement and feelings of wanting to give up, my mentor was there to support. He offered guidance, feedback, and support.

He believed in me when I didn't believe in myself.

I vowed to be the one for the rising leaders with no experience, the leaders who have lost their passion to lead, the leaders at the end of their careers who feel washed up, and the mothers balancing family with leadership careers. Whether you are pulled in five directions or battling your negative inner thoughts, my purpose is to help you develop your unique way of being a better version of yourself than yesterday.

You are not in the boat alone. You are in good company.

I have learned amazing things along my journey. These inexperienced failures have been opportunities for learning and development. I have several scars from these battles, and overall, I am winning the war. You are winning too.

Discovering your passion is an internal journey. Only you will know what lights the fiery furnace within you. Perhaps it is something that only you have the unique skills for or could be uniting under a bigger cause. Let's walk through these five steps to discover your passion.

Five Steps to Discover Your Passion

Step 1: Pulse check. Consider what gets you excited. What motivates your decisions? Is there anything in your life today that results in overwhelming happiness? Is there anything that would cause sadness if it's removed from your life?

Step 2: Core values. What are your core values? Have you really thought about what these are? Some core values include self-discipline, personal development, integrity, diligence, loyalty, commitment, growth mindset, etc. The list can be endless. What speaks to you and is demonstrated through your passion?

Step 3: Look in the mirror. Self-reflect on what brings you the most joy. What makes you happy? What are you good at? Are there things you generally despise doing? What is important here is what you value most, regardless of the value others place on it.

Step 4: Lose track of time. What things cause you to lose track of time or you don't want to stop doing? Passion will not feel like work. You could spend hours doing it and be perfectly content.

Step 5: Get naked. Take a deep look at yourself and get butt-naked honest. The only person impacted is you. Embrace the thing that lights the fire within you. The only one who will place the most value on your passion will always be you.

Finding your passion is the first step in developing grit. Passion is the foundation. Purpose is the fuel that keep you going during the hard times.

Generally, purpose is rooted in selfless ventures. As with servant leadership, the leader feels the leadership purpose is a privilege. Purpose is adding value to the lives you serve as well as your own life. Many times, you will put other's needs above your own. You will put aside your personal needs without feeling jaded because it is what you were put here to do: serving others through leadership.

Let's look at the why or purpose. Purpose is focused and methodical. It is the reason you do what you do. Purpose grounds you in humility when your ego lends to arrogance. It is a deep emotional connection that invests you back to your passion.

The purpose generates resilience within the leader. The continued focus on the purpose enables the leader to recover from failures, develop action plans more efficiently, and demonstrates conviction. Quitting is never an option.

Burnout is a natural concern for any leader. However, burnout is less of a concern for a passionate leader. With purpose, burnout is mitigated by grit through resilience. Gritty leaders know their purpose. They eat it, breathe it, and live it daily. Purpose is conveyed through their honesty in communication. They are unwavering from their commitment despite hardships, setbacks, and adversity. Passionate leaders hold fast to their inner core values and push forward.

Do you know your leadership purpose? If you are struggling with knowing your leadership purpose, the five whys can help you discover. Ask yourself why you lead. Then ask yourself why four additional times. By the fifth why, you will have the root or driving factor behind your reason for leading.

Put structure around your why by crafting a personal

mission statement. Consider your passion, the influence, and impact of your leadership. Personal mission statements will help you articulate your purpose. A thorough understanding of your purpose will help when your team is struggling with understanding the significance of their role.

There are times when you will have team members who struggle with the purpose of their work or tasks. There are five simple steps to help others understand the bigger picture and their impact on the vision.

Five Steps to Discover Your Purpose

Step 1: Compose a meaningful mission statement. People need something to rally around. Having a clear and concise mission statement will help keep focus on the big picture.

Step 2: Connect team members' personal goals to organizational ones. Show the value and personal gain to team members by connecting goals. You are more likely to achieve buy-in when people know their gain.

Step 3: Discover team members' strengths. Showcase individuals' strengths builds confidence within the team by providing a venue for individuals to shine.

Step 4: Develop positive work culture. Positive environments generate more positivity within the team. The optimism cultivates a growth mindset and encourages excellence within the team.

Step 5: Provide regular positive feedback of the team member's direct impact. Positive feedback reassures the team of performance.

Passion is the *what* and purpose is the *why*. Gritty leaders are made through knowing their passion and understanding their purpose. They help others feel connected to something bigger than themselves. They give meaning to everyday mundane jobs. Gritty leaders focus on the present and the team while preparing for the future and showcasing individual talents. Gritty leaders also know how to get brutally honest without saying a word.

BITE OF GRIT

Grit is founded in passion (the what) and purpose (the why).

Reflect upon what is working well and recognize others for their contributions.

Influence is achieved by leaders through demonstrating their authentic belief in what they are trying to achieve.

Trust is gained by demonstrating that the leader's core value system is doing what is in the best interest of the team.

STEP 1 EXERCISE:

Strengthen your grit with Exercise 1 in the <u>GRIT Bootcamp Workbook</u>!

Step 2:

Get Brutally Honest without Saying a Word

Step 2: Get Brutally Honest without Saying a Word

Let your dreams be bigger than your fears and your actions louder than your words.

Anonymous

Have you ever noticed how some people can just move through life and are successful in everything they undertake? They are cool in stressful situations, always rebound stronger from hard times, and master the greatest challenges.

Perhaps you know their personal struggles and jaded background. They strive through challenges where others crumble. They continue to demonstrate success.

Anyone come to mind?

Do you find yourself wondering what they are doing differently?

Do you ever wish you could have one ounce of that coolness? That suave ability to save a life, cure cancer, and still have time to make homemade cookies.

31

Step two is getting brutally honest without saying a word. It is being honest about your struggles and how you continue to thrive. It is reflection and action. It's what pushed you through and your strength. It is knowing your grit.

Yes, you too have demonstrated grit. Don't sell yourself short.

This step is about uncovering the mental strength from within. It begins by understanding mental toughness versus mental strength.

Generally, mental toughness refers to athletes or professionally trained individuals who test their physical strength. These individuals use mental toughness to test the physical limitations of their bodies and mentally push through the limitations.

On the flip side, mental strength is founded in a holistic melting pot of your emotional well-being, past experiences, drive, values, commitment, and response to stress or challenges.

Mental strength is not based upon genetics. It is not based on physical strength or intelligence. Actually, only 30 percent of achievements are due to intelligence. The remaining 70 percent is achieved through passion, commitment, and response to goals. It is the 70 percent that determines the level of mental strength.

Mental strength is not a value that can be recorded. It is not created on a scale that can be measured. Mental strength is personalized. It is self-initiated and self-driven.

It is a secret weapon leveraged by influential leaders. As a servant-leader, mental strength is foundational to grit.

Mental strength is an abstract quality defined by actions. Actions including building people up, blocking negativity, defining clear goals, accepting responsibility, and seeking out growth opportunities. Mental strength is demonstrated through consistency. Consistency generates the tenacity to continue pushing through despite challenges and the odds.

Everyone has a unique view of mental strength.

This is mine.

~~~~~~

My greatest demonstration of mental strength was my quest to become a physician assistant. I learned about the profession as a freshman in college. Instantly, I knew that was my destiny. I was an honor student with 3.8 grade point average.

I hurried up the white tile stairs of the science building, glancing at my watch. Whew! Five minutes to spare!

Arriving at the open dark wood door, I gently knocked. An elderly gentleman with bifocals on the bridge of his nose motioned for me to enter. Silently, he pointed at the chair.

He spent another two minutes scribbling in his charcoal leather journal. I nervously glanced around his office, reading the degrees hanging in the standard matted frames.

His harsh voice brought me back to reality. He peered at me over his plastic red-rimmed bifocals and told me that he was my advisory counselor. His role was to help determine my future career. Then he asked what I wanted to do with my life.

Here we go!

My 19-year-old face lit up as I described my ambitions of becoming a physician assistant. I was prepared. I provided my empirical evidence as to why this was the best decision for me. I described my knowledge of the differences between a nurse practitioner and physician assistant, my high grades, and my passion for medicine. I knew this is what I wanted to do.

He leaned back in his chair and chuckled. "You will never be a PA. The schools and field are way too competitive. Your GPA is not high enough. You will never get into school. You should be a pharmacist."

I was floored and speechless.

Did he just change my career path?

He does not even know me, I thought. Who is he to make this decision? He's supposed to support *my* decision and help me on *my* decided path.

I sank in the hard wooden chair, still speechless. I blinked back tears of my shattered dream. The advisor proceeded to tell me more about this newfound path of pharmacy.

Ten minutes later, I left his office. I walked along the long, scorching concrete sidewalk to student parking. My mind raced that I barely noticed the sweltering Georgia summer sun. I got into my steaming hot, black

Thunderbird and put my head on the steering wheel. I sobbed uncontrollably. It was an ugly sob. It was the my-dreams-are-crushed-my-world-is-destroyed-I'm-a-terrible-student cry. I went home, dragged myself to bed, and cried myself to sleep.

The next morning, I got *mad*.

Who is he to tell me what is best for me? He doesn't even know me, I thought. He did not listen to me.

So I did what every passion-filled teenager does and chased my dream.

In 1999, I applied to physician assistant school with 846 other applicants. We competed for 32 positions in the program. Two months later, I received my rejection letter.

I cried again. It was another ugly cry. My mind raced back to the counselor.

I started to question myself and my abilities. Was he right?

No!

I wiped the tears and focused on my reality. Deep down, I knew I was not ready for professional school—yet. I did not have all my prerequisites or clinical experience. I needed direction on the next best steps.

I contacted the PA school and made an appointment. I drove the eight-hour round trip for a 30-minute appointment with a professor who worked in the program. He discussed my weaknesses and ways to strengthen my application.

In 2000, I went through the same process and rejection. This time without tears. I knew one day that I would be a practicing physician assistant. I could see it. I believed it. I was becoming mentally stronger.

In 2001, I applied for the third time. During the interview process, the panel asked what I would do if I did not get in again this time.

I smiled and said, "I'll see you next year. One day, I will get into PA school and be a practicing physician assistant."

That year, I was accepted. Upon meeting my class of 36, I learned that it was the third time applying for over 70 percent of the class.

I graduated magna cum laude in May 2003.

If I would have not advocated for myself, I would have pursued being a pharmacist. I would be in a job that I hated with limited people interactions and would not feel I am leading with purpose.

This is one of the many examples of mental strength that has defined my character and my life. This was one of the first experiences that defined my mental strength. I refused to give up despite the odds and what others said. I believed in myself. I believed in my dream and visualized working in my profession of choice.

~~~~~

Mental strength develops with the right tools. Become brutally honest without saying a word through defining your mental strength. Look at your actions that show you refuse to give up. Without saying a word, your actions define your mental strength and tenacity. It is the passion that pushes and makes you successful. Look deep within yourself to know how you define mental strength.

BITE OF GRIT

Get brutally honest without saying a word through actions and self-reflection to show your mental strength, which is unique to you.

Reflect upon your holistic melting pot of emotions, experience, drive, values commitment, and response to feed your grit.

Inspire others through building people up, blocking negativity, defining clear goals, accepting responsibility, and growth opportunities.

Tenacity develops through continued push despite challenges and the odds.

STEP 2 EXERCISE:

Strengthen your grit with Exercise 2 in the GRIT Bootcamp Workbook!

Step 3:

Create Effortless Habits and Lose Your Motivation

Step 3: Create Effortless Habits and Lose Your Motivation

If you are persistent, you will get it. If you are consistent, you will keep it.

Anonymous

Have you ever started a New Year's resolution with the usual this-is-my-year mantra?

I'll lose weight. I'll go back to school. I'll find a new job, so you say.

We have all seen it and done it. Then you quit in a few weeks or months into the resolution. It is easy to do, especially when life gets in the way.

Many people start out with high levels of the motivational biochemical dopamine that fuels the excitement of motivation. Dopamine is the fire you feel when first starting a project.

Typically, the New Year's revolutionist mentality is not seen in mentally strong individuals. You rarely see mentally strong leaders set goals to only have the goals fall by the wayside.

Why? How do mentally strong people avoid this downfall?

Step 3 is about creating effortless habits and losing motivation.

Some believe it is rooted in motivation. Motivation is the drive for needs, desires, or action. It is derived from within the individual.

As a mentally strong individual, let's look at my motivation. I have had a long-term battle with exercise. When I'm motivated, I will go to the gym eight days per week, according to my husband. When not motivated, I could go a couple of months without doing the first activity. I am a prime New Year's revolutionist.

Motivation is the desire to achieve a specific goal. Motivation is generally a positive or negative outcome. The desired behavior releases small amounts of the fire-starting dopamine.

For example, if I am receiving positive feedback from my workouts and changes in my body, I am motivated to continue with the action of working out.

Negative feedback can also impact. If I am not seeing changes or say my weight increases, I am motivated to stop the activity.

With this in mind, motivation is discounted as a driver of achieving goals. However, it can be used to jump-start actions toward goals.

Motivation is located deep in the brain in the area that also controls routine behaviors such as eye movement, teeth grinding, emotions, and habits.

Habits and motivation are neighbors in the brain. Mentally strong people leverage the unique relationship and rewire their brains on a success path through consistency.

You don't have to be the most intelligent or the strongest. You just have to be consistent. Consistency will facilitate the development of grit. Consistency provides a path to ensure you are constantly working on your goals and results.

~~~~~~

Mentally strong leaders are consistent. They demonstrate consistency in all activities. There are three top areas to focus on to ensure consistency.

First, *consistency in focus* is the focus on no more than three critical issues per team or individual. Adding more than three focus items will overwhelm the team and divide the attention. Ensure you follow up on the actions and are supportive with feedback. Team members get frustrated when the leader is pushing one initiative and then the initiative falls off the radar.

Next, mental strength is *consistency with behaviors, decisions, and mood.* Consider the individuals with you commonly interact. Do you think about what mood will they be in today? Inconsistency leads to uncertainty and insecurity.

The leader is always on stage. The higher the position, the bigger the stage.

Lastly, mental strength is *consistency with personal brand.* To achieve a stable following, know what you represent. Consider your passion. Wavering from one value proposition to another demonstrates inconsistency in your brand. Inconsistency creates confusion. Over time, no one will follow you because no one will know what you stand for.

Another tool to aid in consistency is daily habits.

~~~~~~

Daily habits are consistent actions. Motivation or willpower is not long lasting and can be lost. Typically, habits are not lost. On average, it takes two months for any new behavior to become a habit. Habits can easily be achieved. For example, some people get up every morning to work out at 5:00 a.m. Other individuals may do the same activity every Friday night.

Grit allows you to lose motivation and create effortless habits.

Is it possible to develop purposeful habits?

Absolutely!

Let's develop habits with purposeful intent.

Developing habits can be achieved through a systematic approach. Imagine having a system to develop the daily habits that set you up for success in your goals.

Behavioral psychologists recommend following the

3R's to develop habits:

- *Reminder* to trigger the routine

- *Routine* to change or develop a new behavior

- *Reward* a personal gain from the routine

Let's break this system down into bite-sized pieces.

Consider something mindless you do every day. Something you know you do daily. Self-care is an easy habit. Most people bathe and brush their teeth daily.

Reminder is the cue that triggers the routine. For example, placing your medication beside your toothbrush is a reminder to take your medication. Having a charger on your nightstand is a reminder to charge your phone nightly. The reminder triggers the routine.

There are endless examples of reminders. These reminders are one way to rewire your brain. The brain forms a new neuropathway linking the reminder to the action.

Over time, the action becomes routine.

What other things do you do daily? Once you identify your natural daily habit, consider how to integrate a new habit by beginning with a reminder.

Routine is a new or changed behavior. You perform a standard routine → see the reminder → perform a new routine → achieve a reward. For example, you brush your teeth at night and notice your medication. You take the medication. You have created a new action. You develop a better state of health. You have created a new habit. It's that simple. The benefit of the new routine is the reward.

The last component of habit making is *reward*. The reward is your personal gain from the new habit. Consider the medication example. You are now taking your medication daily due to the newly formed habit. Your reward is better health related to the condition treated by the medication.

Let's look at a couple more examples:

Goal: Weight loss

Established habit: place your keys on a small table near the door when you come home.

Reminder: place walking shoes by small table.

Routine: see walking shoes, put them on, and go for a walk.

Reward: you've lost weight due to new habit of walking.

Goal: Prioritizing tasks

Established habit: daily team huddles are completed at the huddle blackboard.

Reminder: add defined area on huddle board for priorities.

Routine: review priorities during daily huddles.

Reward: tasks are completed.

The key drivers of habits are that habits are established, mindless acts. Habits are not reliant upon motivation. Motivation is wonderful to get you started and jump-start initiative, but habits keep you going to achieve your goal.

BITE OF GRIT

Goals are jump-started by motivation and completed by daily habits.

Reminder → routine → reward = habit.

Inconsistency leads to uncertainty and insecurity among your team members.

Trust is rooted in consistency in your leadership through focus, brand, and behavior.

STEP 3 EXERCISE:

Strengthen your grit with Exercise 3 in the GRIT Bootcamp Workbook!

Step 4:

Build Your Resilience with Silent Talk

Step 4: Build Your Resilience with Silent Talk

Resilience is knowing that you are the only one that has the power and responsibility to pick yourself up.

Mary Holloway

Look around the room and notice the small electronic advances. As I look around, I notice my blinking clock, my tablet, my running ceiling fan, the hum of the AC unit, and my desk lamp. I faintly hear my clothes dryer running and my dishwasher cycling.

What do you notice when you look around?

All of these electrical luxuries would not be possible without the resilience of one man.

Time and time again, Ben Franklin experimented and discovered another way that did not work in creation of electricity. He never gave up. Eventually, he did create the circuit that lead to a light bulb and later modernized civilization.

How did he not give up?

Ben Franklin demonstrated resiliency. Time and time again, his "failures" as many would define were viewed by him as successes. He viewed the failure as a newfound way that did not work. Then Franklin simply set up a new experiment and tried again. He showed resilience through silent talk—the silent talk of actions.

Step 4 is building resilience through the silent talk of actions.

We have all heard and seen resilience, but what is it, really?

Resilience is a balance of control and commitment. Resilience is the ability to adapt and bounce back.

When the world pushes you down, you get up stronger. Resilience is our ability to bounce back, recover quickly, and not become impaired by past failures. True resilience of a leader is leading in tough times.

The road to leadership is not a destination. It is a journey that is filled with tiny battles. Those scars show your strengths and where you have been. Embrace the scars and wear them proudly.

Resilience leaders focus their energy on where they can impact the most. Resilience leaders commit to their goals and lives. This commitment is visible in personal and professional relationships.

Grit is the constant devotion through strenuously working through challenges, unwavering through adversity, failures, and lack of demonstrating success.

Other attributes of resilience include maintaining a positive image of the future, clearly defined goals, emotional intelligence, and acceptance of responsibility. Through resilience, the ability to overcome setbacks embodies the servant-leader.

~~~~~

Consider the following scenario:

You have worked closely with a top client for several years. You cultivated a strategic partnership that has yielded growth for both the companies. You celebrated victories and stormed over disagreements.

At the end of the day, the collaborative partnership has always proven fruitful for both. Then one day, you receive the call. You are out. Another vendor is in. The remainder of the meeting is to discuss the transition plan.

~~~~~

Situations similar to this occur way too often in the business world. How do you react? Are you the victim? Do you fear the unknown? Regardless of your initial reaction, the goal is to counter adversity with resiliency.

Resilient leaders quickly shift the negativity to an action plan. They refocus the team away from the emotion and on to the productive outcomes.

Resilient leaders focus on control. Think action, not reaction. What is within your control, and what is not?

At the end of the day, you can only control your actions.

You cannot control how someone responds to a specific situation or discussion. As a leader, you convey the information and let it go.

As servant-leaders, we are passionate about our why. We are devoted to our team. With this mindset comes the responsibility of not personalizing the response of the team. It is very easy to internalize and personalize the response and comments of others. Then you feel personally responsible for the individual's happiness and success. Take control and recognize this cycle.

Personalization also falls into the emotional traps of deflation or victimization. One's deeply rooted emotional habits will determine the path.

After a series of wins, a defeat can lead to *deflation* of a leader—the loss of what actions to take next. The leader feels overwhelmed and uncertain of next steps. This is seen in leaders who capture easy wins continuously. Major changes such as strategic focus changes can leave this leader without a solid directional focus.

Victimization is assuming the role of the helpless victim in the face of adversity. Feedback and recommendations of others are dismissed with criticism and closed-mindedness. This is often seen by a leader who has clocked many years with a specific company to find themselves without employment. Generally, these leaders are resistant to change or the new strategic direction, forcing senior leaders to make leadership changes.

Resilient leaders are able to shift the deflation and

victimization reaction to a proactive approach to adversity. They shift to an active and positive mindset. They identified the factors that are within their control and how to make an impact.

The resilience regimen developed by Albert Ellis and Aaron Beck provides a series of questions to facilitate leaders and team members in understanding their natural reactions. By identifying the natural reactions, the leader can refocus on positive thoughts and move toward proactive mindset (Margolis & Stoltz, 2010).

Here are examples of refocusing and moving toward positive and proactive mindset:

- Natural reaction: what could have been done to prevent the event?

- Positive mindset: what can I do now to improve the situation?

- Natural reaction: what is the cause of the event?

- Positive mindset: what positive impact can I bring now?

- Natural reaction: is the cause a local or widespread effect?

- Positive mindset: what can I do today to address the problem?

- Natural reaction: is the cause temporary or long term?

- Positive mindset: what can I do today to address the

problem?

Resilience is learned over time. It is developed over the times of stress and challenges faced. As with control, resilience is also balanced with commitment. Commitment in your approach to daily, chronic, and situational stress. Use the mnemonic REAL to strengthen resilience and refocus energy when facing situational stress (Klein, PhD & Bowman, 2013).

R=Relationships

E=Efficacy

A=Attitude

L=Learning

Relationships are a key factor in developing resilience. Everyone needs someone as a close confidante. This individual will support you in times of difficulty. He or she will motivate you when you have lost your will. He or she will keep you engaged and focused. In a high-value relationship, you can count on him or her for feedback and to call you out when you make a bad decision.

Efficacy is related to developing goals and the belief that you can achieve your goals. Resilience is knowing what you can control and that your actions make a difference. Celebrating accomplishments and wins will develop your confidence and mental strength. Start thinking about your goals and the accomplishments you have achieved.

Attitude represents your approach toward challenges or

stress. Positivity provides a mental environment for creativity, problem solving, and increased coping skills. Positivity reflects emotions such as happiness, optimism, and gratitude. Consider the individuals or things that give you pure joy. Reflect on this in challenges.

Learning represents the lessons you learn through challenges. While it can be difficult, consider the learning process throughout the challenges and times of stress. What are the supporting factors that lead to your decisions? Reflect upon your most challenging decisions over the past couple of weeks. How did it affect others? What were the downstream impact? Would you make the same decision again?

Gritty leaders build resilience with silent talk through refusing to give up on goals. Through resilience, you too continue to rise up. Recognize each trial as an opportunity for discovery and enlightenment even though it may not yield the desired results. Shift from reactions to action plans in times of adversity and resist the role of victim.

BITE OF GRIT

Gritty leaders counter adversity with resilience.

Resilience is the ability to adapt, bounce back, recover quickly, and not become impaired by past failures.

Identify factors that are within your control to change

and will yield the biggest impact.

Treat each situation as a resilience-building opportunity through the REAL steps (Relationship, Efficiency, Attitude, Learning).

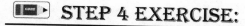 ## STEP 4 EXERCISE:

Strengthen your grit with Exercise 4 in the <u>GRIT Bootcamp Workbook</u>!

Step 5:

How to Control Your Emotions to Avoid Bad Decisions

Step 5: How to Control Your Emotions to Avoid Bad Decisions

Good decisions come from experience, and experience comes from bad decisions.

Anonymous

Imagine presenting a report to your manager. You put in tons of hours and hard work. You pushed outside your comfort zone. You presented your masterpiece and was received with criticism and negative feedback. Angrily, you storm back to your office and stew over the comments—what did they mean by amateur work? Do they not realize I'm a seasoned veteran in my field? I don't have time to redo it!

At some point in life, many have experienced something similar. I tend to think of this as a significant emotional event. It is triggered by the passion felt for the task being performed.

Step 5 is how to control your emotions and avoid bad decisions.

Self-awareness will help diffuse the anger. Begin diffusing anger with these steps detailed by Christine A. Padesky:

1. Calm yourself: deep breathing, meditation.
2. State your current situation: state only the facts.
3. Identify your mood in one word: angry, sad, frustrated, humiliated, insecure.
4. Acknowledge your natural reaction: doesn't like me, skills not good enough, rude and arrogant.
5. Find objective supporting evidence: what supports your thoughts?
6. Define objective contradictory evidence: what contradicts your natural reactions?
7. Think fair and balanced thoughts.
8. Monitor present mood: create affirmations.

Avoiding emotionally based bad decisions begins with control. Mentally strong leaders demonstrate emotional control.

Perhaps this has not been your strong suit in the past. You have identified passion with emotion. These can easily be confused. Passion is your reason what and the core of your aspiration to lead. It is the fuel of your desire, and your purpose will hold you steadfast in hard times. Passion also generates overwhelming and deep-seated emotions.

Controlling emotions begins with recognizing factors within your control. Natural disasters such as earthquakes are out of your control. The way you manage through the disaster aftermath is within your control.

Control is a symbol of self-confidence. Self-confidence is having a sense of one's life purpose. Control is the power over something such as a person, process, or even oneself. Control is personal influence.

Mentally strong individuals demonstrate resilience through focusing energy on situations or events they can influence. Servant-leaders are empowered by the ability to influence and modify outcome.

Focusing on uncontrolled circumstances will drain your energy. The lack of control will leave you feeling hopeless, powerless, and lost. The lack of focus will translate to your team impacting your leadership.

Control is not achieved by dwelling on the past events without modifiable factors. Past events are history. They are out of one's power to change. Dwelling on the past leads to regret and second-guessing. Dwelling on past decisions will result in stunted personal growth. Dwelling is being stuck in the mental replay of the situation without insights. Instead, leverage self-reflection. When thinking of the past, replay the situation and understand the mindset that resulted in the situation. Self-reflection promotes personal growth through insights that yielded the situational results.

What were the circumstances that factored into the decision?

Who were the key players?

What were the options available?

What was the downstream effect of the decision?

Ultimately, understanding the why and how behind the decision will foster professional growth. Mentally file these insights away and use the newfound knowledge to provide insights for future decision.

Control is also achieved by knowing one's weakness.

It takes a strong person to act in humility and an even stronger leader to know one's weakness. Acting with humility is the foundation of respect between the leader and the follower. Humility is an acknowledgement of your weaknesses. You must be able to look honestly in the mirror and recognize your shortcomings.

Humility is not a sign of weakness or permissiveness. It is not over or under-valuing one's worth. Humility does not equate to low self-esteem or self-defeating behavior. Lastly, it is not an avenue to self-degeneration.

Humility is the simple act of being a humble leader. It is letting go of your ego and putting others' needs before your own. Humility is taking the higher road and completing actions for the greater good instead for personal gain. It is a venue of effective leadership.

Everyone has a bad day and longs for the opportunity of a do-over. The reality is all these poor decisions and obvious mistakes are an opportunity for professional growth. It is through these bad days that you will grow professionally and gain experience of how to best respond to future situations. It cultivates foresight of the leader.

Foresight is used to guide the servant-leader through learning from the past, mindfulness of the present, and understanding the potential consequences of the future. It provides a venue for the leader to anticipate questions and responses for future meetings. Thus, the leader will be better prepared mentally for the next challenge. Mental toughness is shifting from reaction-driven to foresight-driven leadership.

Mental toughness is the ability to recognize it's not always about you. The questions, the responses, and the actions are not a reflection of you as an individual. These interactions are responses to the situation.

It's business, not personal.

As a servant-leader, you leverage qualities such as coping, motivation, confidence and consistency. Mentally tough teams are created through the leader's ability to cultivate a culture of trust, inclusion, and humility. The team members have a stronger connection with the team as well as the leader. A culture of trust creates an environment of tenacity and perseverance that carry the individuals through adversity.

Mental toughness is remaining optimistic when faced with adversity. One defeat does not equate to complete failure. At some point, everyone loses. Nothing is gained in victory. Defeat provides an opportunity for growth and evolution. Guide the team on character, consistency, and self-reflection. You must continue to build your team up over and over again.

As a servant-leader, you lead from the heart. It is the passion for leadership and serving others that provides satisfaction in everyday tasks. The strong sense of empathy provides a venue for connecting with team members. The dark side of empathy is how it creeps into our subconscious and allows others to influence emotions.

Consider a situation where everyone jumps on a bandwagon. One comment leads to a ripple effect. One day everything is sunshine and roses. The next day, the company is perceived as failing apart. You begin questioning yourself on your leadership decisions: How did I not see that coming? How could I make such a dumb and obvious mistake?

Simple. Influence of emotions.

Mental toughness stems from the ability to leverage empathy yet separate our emotions from the present situation. The leader became caught up in the rapid firing of questions and was emotionally connected to the project. Having identified so closely with the project, the questions were internalized. The defensive responses were in feeling that others were undermining and discounting the work.

Others will always try to bring you down. It is human nature, and many individuals don't perceive the impression of their own actions. Consider these ill comments as tiny tests of your mental strength.

At the end of the day, will these comments or actions impact you in one year?

No! You will forget it, as you should do. Stop wasting

your energy.

Don't allow the influence of a failed situation to cause you to lose control. Have the courage and the mental toughness to take a deep breath and manage. Don't allow the emotions to distract you from doing what needs to be done.

~~~~~

As a leader, you are always on stage. Allowing emotions to take over will place questions into other's minds of your ability to lead. Consider the last time you witnessed leaders losing their composure. Did they scream or raise their voice? How did you feel watching this event?

Loss-of-composure situations can be unsettling for anyone to witness, especially a direct report or team member. Keep in mind the stage. The higher the position, the bigger the stage. Control your emotions, or you will have a Broadway show on your stage.

How do you gain control of your emotions?

Follow these five simple steps to gain mental toughness and to control your emotions:

1. Control emotions in the moment

Emotionally based decisions generate no benefit to the team nor showcase your best leadership traits. Be cognizant of your physical response when you become emotionally stimulated. Often these physical signs are anxiety, increased heart rate, nausea, sweaty hands, and flushing of skin.

You must develop the foresight to recognize when you are going down this path. Stop and refocus. Take charge of your breathing. Think about your happy place. Regain the control your emotion has on the situation. Control yourself in the moment.

2. Identify productive ways of handling emotions

Studies suggest that we are a product of our environment. It is shown in the way we subconsciously learn to manage emotions. Think back to your childhood and how the family figures of your life managed stress. Can you identify some similarities? Which emotion was the most uncomfortable? If these thoughts are difficult to you, you may need to seek professional assistance.

Replay the situations in your mind. How could you have responded to the situation differently? How would you respond with empathy and without emotion now? Sometimes it is helpful to discuss these situations with an objective colleague. Do some role-playing. A trusted colleague can provide a different perspective.

3. Reflect on your feelings

As a servant-leader, you leverage self-awareness to represent and know your true self, your openness to suggestion, and the impact of your emotions on the team. To understand your emotional impact, begin by giving your emotions structure. These intrinsic negative emotions include

- Sadness: sad, blue, alone, lonely

- Hostility: anger, hostility, irritability, scorn, loathing, disgust

- Fear: anxious, afraid, frightened, nervous, shaky, jittery

- Guilt: blameworthiness, self-anger, shame

By creating a structure of the emotion, you begin to develop more self-awareness. You will recognize the emotion as it emerges and be able to quickly negate the emotion from taking control over you. Also, challenge yourself to unveil the cause of these negative thoughts of fear, inadequacy, and complex emotion. What is the trigger?

4. Responding to your negative emotions

When reflecting on the situation, consider the facts. As a leader, you make decisions based on the facts. What evidence supports or refutes the trigger of your emotion? Negative emotions can impact a leader's decision-making ability. By understanding the cause of the emotion, you can better manage the reactions and thus avoid making a bad decision.

To begin, identify the negative thoughts. You may find that journaling is a helpful tool. Reflect on your feelings and identify the intrinsic negative emotions above. Now you must stop the negative thoughts. Counteract the negative thought with a positive one. Start with negative word substitution. Here are a few examples of negative work substitutions:

- Disaster → challenge
- Change → opportunity
- Terrible → not what I hoped for
- Never → let's try

These simple modifications will pave your way to controlling negative emotions. You are leveraging your growth mindset. Consider how to start thinking of the glass as half full instead of half empty.

5. Leverage regulation techniques

Being pushed outside your comfort zone is a huge professional growth opportunity. This discomfort generates uncertainty and negative emotions. This uncertainty could lead you to make poor decisions due to the fear of failure. Recognize the uncertainty and develop tolerance. Take time to recognize the discomfort as an opportunity and leverage regulation techniques to manage uncertainty.

Regulation techniques would include mindfulness, whereby you are fully conscious in the moment. Additional techniques would include meditation, yoga, nature walk, hot baths, or physical activity. The key is identifying the regulation technique that works best for you.

At some point in your leadership, you will make a bad

decision or regrettable mistake. If you are not making bad decisions, you are not taking risks to grow the team, yourself, and the business. Analyze the bad decision, assess the damage, and institute the backup plan. Your ability to respond promptly with an appropriate action plan is what will set you apart as a great leader.

The key to understanding how to avoid making bad decisions is control through self-awareness. Operate with a high level of emotional intelligence and empathy. Know your people and their experience. Do not pretend to share similar experiences if you have not. Pretending to experience something you have not is mimicry, not empathy. People will see this and become resentful. Be mindful of your emotions, also known as gut instinct. Control the emotion to avoid making emotionally driven bad decisions.

BITE OF GRIT

Gritty leaders shift from reaction-driven to foresight-driven leadership.

Recognize negative personal emotions and counteract with positive emotion substitution.

Influence of others' emotions or bad outcomes can distract keeping you from leading. Have courage, take a deep breath, and manage.

Tenacity and perseverance are developed in a culture of trust. Carry individuals through adversity.

STEP 5 EXERCISE:

Strengthen your grit with Exercise 5 in the GRIT Bootcamp Workbook!

Step 6:

WARNING: Self-Sabotage and Imposter Syndrome—Are You a Victim?

Step 6: WARNING: Self-sabotage and Imposter Syndrome—Are You a Victim?

It's not who you think you are that holds you back, it's who you think you are not.

Anonymous

At some point along human development, everyone has experienced negative self-talk:

What are you *thinking*? You cannot do this!

You will fail, so why try?

You aren't good enough. You are not strong, smart, or fast enough.

Sound familiar? It is a completely normal part of human development.

Step 6 is recognizing the personal victimization of self-sabotage and imposter syndrome.

Self-sabotage is deliberately destroying, damaging, or obstructing with purposeful intent. It has no rational reason. For many individuals, it just happens. You are pushing forward, and suddenly, you come to a screeching halt.

Sound familiar? Take the **Self-Sabotage Quiz** to find out if you are your own worst enemy. The quiz will help you identify if you are a Self-Sabotage Champion, Warrior, or Trooper. After the quiz, you will discover my personal favorite resources for muffling your inner critic or taking your strength to the next level!

What's the trigger?

Often, it is the misalignment of one's self-image comparisons to our goal. This misalignment sends a signal to the brain to rebel. The rebellion causes mental self-destruction known as self-sabotage.

What do you tell yourself when you do not achieve a goal? How about when you feel it is due to failure? Do you unknowingly begin with self-sabotage?

Ever known people who fall off the wagon? Have you questioned why? They worked so hard to reach their goal and now are worse than when they started.

What leads to this destructive behavior?

Too often, we are the tyrant of self-targeted sabotage. The behavior comes without warning. One small mishap can leave you doubting all your skills.

There are some common themes found in self-sabotage (Mind Tools, 2018). These devil-like themes have a mission of destroying your self-confidence. Themes include:

Self-Sabotage: Worry and Control

The worry theme shows when individuals are consumed about things in general. They worry about failure, doubting personal ability, and what others think. They worry about deadlines, project alignment, and budgets. Many times, it spills over into their personal life, thus worrying about spouse, marriage, and family. Many develop anxiety, panic attacks, and depression attempting to achieve their goal.

The worry is often attributed to loss of control. The loss of control is letting go of the situation. Letting go can be scary for the control-minded leader. As leaders, our goal is to trust and empower. Subconsciously, it is easier to self-destruct rather than trust others and risk something spinning out of control.

Recognize your personal tendencies. Understand your temperament and where you feel the onset of anxiety. Rewire your brain from thinking of losing control and into empowerment of the team. Be confident in your abilities and less worried about the things outside your control.

Self-Sabotage: Self-Worth

Self-worth is rooted in self-confidence. Low self-confidence will give an internal feeling of worthlessness. Worthlessness is seen when others downplay their personal success while emphasizing the success of others. Worthlessness is giving someone else power to put you down or harvesting the power to put yourself down.

Don't let these self-destructive thoughts contaminate your soul. Recognize self-destructive thoughts as poison.

How do you receive feedback or constructive criticism? Have you been told you wear your heart on your sleeve?

Self-sabotage will leave you taking the criticism to heart. Consider feedback as a gift. Someone is taking the time to provide guidance on ways you can do things *differently* to achieve a greater outcome.

Notice I've said do things *differently*.

The mental shift to feedback as a gift was a milestone for me along my journey. Early in my career, I subconsciously began refuting the feedback. Believing that it was due to others' shortcomings, I provided excuses for mine. I had a fixed mindset.

Once I realized my fixed mindset, I began developing internal stops when I started the defensive rebuttals.

Through the development of others, servant-leaders harness grit of those led through fostering a growth mindset. The growth mindset allows feedback to be processed differently. When I embraced a growth mindset, a mental shift evolved. I rewired my thoughts to consider feedback differently and as a gift.

The feedback became an opportunity for professional growth, not self-destruction. Someone is sharing their expertise and observations on how to be a better version of me! I began embracing that thought. Once I did, my performance increased significantly.

Change your mindset from viewing feedback as criticism. It is an opportunity for growth and a way to achieve a better result. You will build self-confidence and self-worth.

Self-Sabotage: Imposter Syndrome

The imposter syndrome is the perception that you do not possess the skills or knowledge required to perform a task or job. It is deeply rooted in self-worth and confidence. Perhaps you are faced with a new task and unsure of your skills. You doubt yourself and attempt to go unnoticed. You feel like an imposter. You rise to a higher position, realizing later it can be a greater fall.

Seventy percent of individuals will experience the imposter syndrome during their work life (Estacio, PhD, 2018).

The majority of us have experienced self-sabotage. Today is the day to cultivate your mental strength and pull yourself up by your bootstraps. If you are caught in the trap of self-destruction, *The Imposter Syndrome Remedy* book by Dr. Emee Estacio is a way to disrupt your fixed mindset.

Self-Sabotage: Familiarity

Familiarity brings comfort and security. Familiarity keeps you in your comfort zone. Many leaders are afraid of the unknown. Pushing outside your comfort zone brings fear, anxiety, and loss of control and security. Change is scary for many.

It is easier to maintain the status quo and keep a low profile. This is often seen in domestic violence. The individual knows the relationship is unhealthy but continues to return. The relationship is familiar. The downfall of familiarity is stagnant growth. You will fall into the rut of repeat low-quality decisions.

Start today and change your mindset. Recognize the attraction to your comfort zone. Growth only occurs when you are willing to step outside your comfort zone. If you continue with the status quo, then you will continue to deliver with same results.

Self-Sabotage: Anger

Anger is a powerful emotion in self-sabotage. It can destroy relationships with coworkers, family, friends, and clients. Passive-aggressive communication is a common symptom of anger.

Anger can be disguised as jealousy or resentment. It is easy to be jealous of someone's success. The why-not-me thoughts slowly start creeping in. Don't be resentful or jealous of another's success. Celebrate it. Collaborate with the individual. Your growth mindset will facilitate your colleagues' celebration of their success.

Don't fall victim to the downfall of anger.

Self-sabotage is rooted in fear of failure. It is the paralyzing fear of doing your absolute best yet failing. It is the fear of being humiliated and losing your self-worth. It is the perception that your best simply doesn't measure up to standard.

If any of these self-sabotaging themes are controlling you and holding you from moving forward, consider getting additional help such as counseling. Many times, counseling can reveal the underlying cause of the behavior and provide a venue to move forward. Counseling is another way to push you out of your comfort zone and develop mental strength. If you are stuck, get help.

Now the balance becomes how to align your conscious and your subconscious to push forward to meet the goal. In a way, it is how to hack the brain to achieve the goal. It is centered on self-talk.

~~~~~

Remember the story about the small train going up the mountain? Every train doubted the little train's ability to succeed. The little train repeated, "I think I can" several times until she went over the mountain.

While many of our daily challenges are far more complex than completing a simple task, lots can be learned by the positive thinking displayed in the story. The character believed she would be successful. She visualized herself achieving her goal. She conveyed it through positive thoughts and visualization.

Are you a positive or negative thinker?

Failure is often rooted in negative thinking. You may not be a victim of self-sabotage but exhibit negative thinking. For example, you know you have the skills, yet still have a reason the task cannot be performed. Negative thoughts subconsciously give you permission to quit— permission to stop focusing on your goals. Negative thoughts are distractors. Stop focusing on what you have not accomplished and celebrate what you have accomplished. Get ready to change.

Changing the negative self-talk into positive self-talk is foundational of mentally strong individuals. We are not our thoughts. The things that play rerun in our minds are not us. We choose to feel irrelevant, hopeless, lost, and insecure. We also choose to feel significant, hopeful, inspired, and powerful. It takes just as much energy to feel either way. The choice is yours.

Positive and negative thoughts are founded in our subconscious. The thoughts reflect the ability or perceived inability of completing a task or goal. Negative thoughts will often creep in and out before we are aware. The damage to our subconscious is already done. Negative thoughts will often result in failure.

Mentally strong leaders break the task into smaller, more manageable tasks. These quick tasks are quick wins. The quick wins are the positive feedback and tasks that achieve the overall goal. Positive thoughts of goal completion will oftentimes lead to successfully achieving the goal.

Take a moment to consider your thought process regarding any goal. Let your thoughts just flow. You can use the template in Exercise 6 of the workbook as a guide.

As you assess your thoughts, what do you notice? Any patterns? Try not to make general assumptions. Making one mistake at your job does not mean you are bad at your job. Your overall performance is not defined by one mistake. So don't allow the mistake to define you.

While you may not have definite self-sabotaging thoughts, your thoughts may be rooted in negativity.

Mentally strong individuals have faith in their abilities. They exhibit positive and optimistic thoughts. They are willing to invest in hard work and adjust course when needed. They refuse to be victims of self-sabotage.

Now look at your thought pattern again. Do you see any general themes?

Self-sabotage is often a misalignment between goals and reality. Themes of self-sabotage include worry, control, self-worth, fraudulence, familiarity, and anger. Failure is often rooted in negative thinking. Break large tasks into smaller ones for quick wins.

BITE OF GRIT

Get a new view, as making a mistake does not equate to being bad at your job, so don't allow the mistake to define you.

Recognize self-destructive thoughts as mental poison that can contaminate your soul.

Imposter syndrome is experienced by 70 percent of individuals and is exacerbated by higher-level leadership positions.

Thoughts that play rerun in our minds may not represent our ability, as it takes just as much energy to have negative thoughts as positive thoughts.

STEP 6 EXERCISE:

Strengthen your grit with Exercise 6 in the GRIT Bootcamp Workbook!

Step 7:

Do Stress Differently

Step 7: Do Stress Differently

*Working hard for something we
don't care about is called stress.
Working hard for something we
love is called passion.*

Anonymous

Stress is your natural response to danger or threat. It leads to a powerful release of neurochemicals initiating a fight-or-flight response. Remember that pounding heart, profuse sweating, and gut-wrenching fear?

That feeling is related to adrenaline, cortisol, and norepinephrine. What about the little nervous giggle? It is the body's subconscious effort to release dopamine and drives down the nervousness.

Remember the last project that stretched you beyond your limits? The fear of potentially failing?

You pushed outside your comfort zone. Full of trembles and anxiety, you took a deep breath and pushed forward. What happened? You succeeded. You pushed beyond your limits and what you imagined.

Step 7 is understanding how to do stress differently and harness stress to your benefit.

Aside from the personal reason of improving our quality of life, stress management is vital to the sustainability of the team. People cannot continue to function in a pressure-cooker environment. Eventually, people burn out.

~~~~~

In a recent study by Kronos Incorporated, 95 percent of HR managers have a workplace plagued by employee burnout. Nearly all managers are feeling the impact (Maroney, 2017).

The top three reasons contributing to burnout include poor compensation at 41 percent, excessive hours at 32 percent, heavy workload at 32 percent, poor management at 30 percent, role confusion at 29 percent, and negative environment at 26 percent.

Employee burnout leads to increased turnover, which can be a good thing. The benefit is fresh blood and eyes on the team. The team is reinvigorated with new ideas. Beware that this does come at a cost. The cost associated with turnover from the view of training is about 60 to 200 percent of annual salary.

To help combat the rising cost, organizations need to be willing to recruit for top performers as well as reinvest in their current top performers. This can disrupt the churn cycle and cultivate greater leaders within the newfound environment.

~~~~~

There are other pain points resulting in burnout. Identifying and managing of the causes of burnout rejuvenates the team.

Are your days filled with endless conference calls, meetings, or emails? You are busy with calls while the Outlook pop-ups are reminding you of other demands. The extra hours to achieve zero inbox have been quickly sabotaged with fifty new emails demanding your attention.

Why is this the new norm?

Technology-driven instant information culture is often the result of too many decision makers. Each decision maker must be heard and be in line with the final decision. The priorities become blurred, and initiatives fall short of expectations through the excessive collaboration model. This heightened level of collaboration is filling employee schedules with nonproductive meetings and monopolizing their time with senseless email replies.

As the leader, consider the decision makers. Excessive decision makers act more as speed bumps and slow the advancements of initiatives. Examine the number of meetings within the organization. What can be eliminated? Giving time back to the employees will provide a way to reinvest the time into innovation.

Burnout can also be attributed to increased workload. Most often the high performers are victims of heavier workloads. These are the ones who you can count on to help relieve some of your own excessive workload. Perhaps you sell the extra work as stretch assignments or growth opportunities. Be fair and don't take advantage of hard workers. Be mindful of workloads, especially with your high performers.

~~~~~

Consider this scenario:

I wonder what's going on with Alice. She hasn't been the same since our large project. She's having trouble completing her work, drifting in meetings, and so negative. Everything is wrong and has issues. Alice just does not seem happy. It is like she has lost her spark.

I heard her blood pressure has been elevated and her doctor placed her on medication.

~~~~~

Do you know the signs of burnout?

As a leader, you must recognize and home in on the signs of burnout. Recognizing the signs will help you intervene and provide support to the team members (Gerry, 2013).

Burnout can be demonstrated as exhaustion. This exhaustion can be exhibited as physical, mental, or emotional. It is a general feeling of overall fatigue.

Exhaustion is followed by lack of motivation. It could be difficulty getting out of bed or starting the day. Draining motivation is also shown through loss of enthusiasm.

Over time, this loss of motivation is overshadowed by negativity. Negativity manifests as cynicism, frustration, and anger. While these are all normal emotions, it is important to recognize when it becomes excessive.

Burnout can also be seen through difficulty focusing. Does your mind wander during meetings? Do you have difficulty with recalling details? Reduced focus is the brain's way of compartmentalizing the stress.

Poor performance is often a telltale sign of burnout. Consider your past performance. Have you noticed a decline, especially among your team members?

Burnout can manifest as personal problems. These problems can be seen at work or at home. The individual may have more arguments or become withdrawn.

Coping mechanisms of problems may be seen through lack of personal care. You may notice the individual is coping with food, alcohol, smoking, lack of exercise, or even self-medication.

The lack of self-care will evolve into health problems. Over time, chronic stress can result in heart disease, obesity, anxiety, and depression.

It is okay to lose your spark from time to time. It is okay to fall down. When you get up, rage as the whole blazing fire and harness your power.

Can you harness the power of stress without the negative effects? Yes, you can! Imagine having the intense power of stress to steer to your desired direction.

How?

By stress busting!

According to Harvard Business Review, professional athletes and Navy SEALs rely on a simple three-step process to response to stress. The approach minimizes the negative effects and maximizes the positive outcomes (Crum & Crum, 2015).

Stress Transformation Steps

Step 1: Name the Stress

Take charge of stress before it takes charge of you. What is the origin of the stress? Start a sentence with "I'm stressed about _____ (fill in the blank)."

Research shows the simple step of labeling the cause of the stress transitions the brain from reactive to proactive (Crum & Crum, 2015).

Thinking through your actions will help understand your overall response to stressful situations.

Step 2: Own It

The things that matter the most to you will induce the most stress in your life. What do you value? What do you represent?

Owning the stress will provide the motivation to carry you through the hard times. If leadership was easy, everyone would be the boss.

Owning the stress means you have made the choice to

embrace it as part of your journey. It is your decision to have stress, and you control the level of intensity.

Step 3: Use It

Stress triggers the neurochemicals dopamine and adrenaline. These chemicals create a natural high and increase awareness of the body and brain.

Here's a ninja trick! Rewire your brain to see anxiety as excitement. The newfound excitement can enhance performance.

In addition to the stress-busting steps, you should recognize the types of stress. Generally, there are four different types of stress: time, anticipatory, situational, and encounter (Mind Tools, 2018). Each type of stress can be combated with a quick tool found in Exercise 7 of your GRIT Bootcamp Workbook.

Time Stress

This is stress centered on time or lack thereof. You feel overwhelmed by number of tasks compared to time to accomplish. Common examples include deadlines, being late, or missed meetings.

> ➢ **Secret tool:** a to-do list will help prioritize your tasks, ensuring that you spend the appropriate time on each item.

Anticipatory Stress

This is stress centered on the future such as an upcoming event. This stress can also be vague such as a feeling of doom. Generally, anticipatory stress is rooted in fear of failure or lack of confidence.

> ➤ **Secret tool:** Use a decision tree. A decision tree is a systemic way of weighing options in a decision. It will outline the potential effects and options of your decision. Also, it will help you think through the downstream impacts of the decision.

Situational Stress

This is stress centered on an unforeseen situation. Conflict is a common cause of situational stress. Imagine sitting in a meeting that erupts into a shouting match. Individuals with heightened stress will feel withdrawn and have difficulty interacting in that environment.

> ➤ **Secret tool:** Use a conflict resolution map. A conflict resolution map will help understand the drivers of the conflict and facilitate the resolution.

Encounter Stress

This is stress centered on the interactions with specific people. This could stem from the individual's unpredictability or a simple personality conflict.

> ➤ **Secret tool:** SWOT yourself. SWOT analysis can be useful for identifying your personal strength,

weaknesses, opportunities, and threats. By identifying your SWOT, you can showcase your strengths and develop your weaknesses.

Everyone experiences stress at some point in life. It could be related to heavy traffic, workload, family, or news stress. The majority of stress is manageable.

When stress is not manageable, it can impact you by way of simple daily productivity and your health over time. A stress diary is one tool to help identify stress situations and responses.

Stress management is vital to the quality of life and preventing employee burnout. Burnout can be attributed to poor compensation, excessive hours, heavy workload, poor management, role confusion, and negative environment. Signs of burnout include exhaustion, lack of motivation, negativity, difficulty focusing, poor performance, personal problems, lack of personal care, and health problems. Recognize these signs and help your team do stress differently.

BITE OF GRIT

Gritty leaders rewire their brain to harness the power of stress into newfound excitement to enhance performance.

Rewire your response to stress with a three-stage

approach: 1. Name the stress. 2. Own the stress. 3. Use the stress.

Identify signs of burnout such as exhaustion, lack of motivation, negativity, difficulty focusing, poor performance, personal problems, lack of personal care, and health problems.

Types of stress include time, anticipatory, situational, and encounter stress.

STEP 7 EXERCISE:

Strengthen your grit with Exercise 7 in the GRIT Bootcamp Workbook!

Step 8:

Make This Commitment

That Will

Change Your Life

Step 8: Make This Commitment That Will Change Your Life

Before you are a leader, success is all about growing yourself. When you become a leader, success is all about growing others.

Jack Welch

Have you ever read the story of Steve Jobs? Steve was a pioneer at Apple. He developed significant advancements in the technology industry. One day, the board felt it was time for him to exit the company.

Apple almost went bankrupt. Apple brought Steve back. Jobs returned stronger and with more innovation than ever demonstrated. Today, the simplistic design and user-friendly functionality dominate the industry.

Jobs exhibited resilience.

Resilient individuals dust themselves off after hardships and come back stronger.

Why?

Gritty individuals are committed. Grit commits to

making dreams a reality. Through a driving passion, Steve Jobs committed to making the best product in the industry.

Step 8 is about making the one commitment that will change your life. It begins with understanding the value to commitment. It is the commitment to yourself for personal development.

Commitment is shown though the approach to one's goals. Mentally strong people set SMART goals as previously described. They create actions around the goals and drive until the goal is achieved. Mental strength will establish the dedication to achieve the goal. Servant-leaders achieve success through dedication.

Have you ever heard the phrase nothing comes easily?

Generally, it is true.

The quick and easy path can yield quick wins and instant results. Unfortunately, the majority of the time, these results are often short lived. Consider the fads of days past—bell bottoms, platform shoes, top hats, and bow ties. Just like fashion trends, shortcuts are not sustainable.

The most important commitment you can make to developing grit is the commitment to you and your personal development. This single commitment will change your life. The commitment to personal development will forever place you on a path of growth and potential success. It is the power to invest in long-term success.

A gap is created by what is achieved and the potential of what can be achieved. Without effort and passion, the gap widens as unmet potential and loss.

To close the unmet gap, the servant-leader develops one's interest and skills. The leader pushes the envelope and barrels through plateaus. The leader sees the potential in the ones led and guides them along their journey.

For you and others, commitment starts with creating appropriate and outcome-based goals. Upon setting a goal, the brain changes. It integrates the goal into self-image. If the image isn't aligned to the goal, the brain works to achieve it.

How cool is that? Your brain is programmed to help you achieve your goal!

Along the way, the brain rewards for the small victories toward the goal by releasing dopamine, which stimulates happiness.

Consider the last time someone shared with you a small victory:

Hey, I lost three pounds!

Look! I ran half a mile!

Wow! I can finally send an email!

Do you recall the excitement in his or her voice? Physiologically, it is the microinjection of dopamine fueling their excitement. The flowing chemical produces a biological drug-induced happiness.

Neurohack this victory-inducing chemical by setting several short-term goals to achieve long-term goals.

Celebrate the achievements—big or small!

What happens when you fail to meet the goal?

You are punished—by your brain.

The brain identifies the misalignment of the self-image and the goal. Dopamine and serotonin levels drop. Cortisol increases rapidly. You feel stressed out, irritable, sad, disappointed, and have an overall feeling of loss. Essentially, you grieve the loss of achieving the goal.

You may develop the automatic self-destructive behavior in steps. By now, you recognize these negative thoughts. Call them untruths. Put these untruths in a box and throw away the key.

Refuse to give your leadership power to these tiny self-destructive lies. Recognize them and take back your power.

Consider the kid who missed the winning ball.

The lost account or client.

Missing the last flight that would get you home in time for an important family event.

Wow! Now my dopamine levels are dropping!

How do you ensure you can meet your goals and continue to ride the wave of happiness?

Simple.

Set goals and make them SMART:

S=Specific: what would you like to achieve?

M=Measurable: how will you know you are successful?

A=Achievable: what steps will you take?

R=Relevant: can you describe your perfect world?

T=Time-bound: when do you see yourself reaching your goal?

Do you have a goal in mind? Okay, great! Now cut that goal in half.

Yes, that's right! Take that huge, hairy, audacious goal and cut it in half.

Why? Generally, goals are created when you are the most motivated. You are inspired and ready to conquer the world. Cutting the goal in half will lead to small victories on your way to accomplish that huge, hairy, audacious goal.

Next, get a pen and paper. Go ahead and grab it if you aren't taking notes. Now write the goal down. When you write down the goal, the goal becomes real. It is tangible. It is living.

Let's look at an example.

GOAL: Becoming a better communicator is a common and critical goal of every leader.

Communication is vague and broad. Let's put some structure around it using the SMART technique:

GOAL: Deliver quarterly verbal presentations to senior leadership that are related to updates that are clear and comprehensive.

Great! It meets all the SMART criteria. How will we measure again the goal to show progression? Think about this one on how you will measure success. For the verbal communication goal, we could use the following:

- Mass feedback survey after the meeting

- Asking leaders for individual feedback

Now let's cut that goal in half:

GOAL: Deliver monthly verbal presentation to direct manager that's related to clear and comprehensive updates.

This small change of cutting the goal in half will increase my chances of success. With my direct manager, I will be practicing my verbal skills, learning my comprehensive material, and eliciting feedback, which I can implement in real time.

Consider the goals, make them SMART, and write them down.

The single life-changing commitment is the commitment to yourself through continuous development.

As with many professions, continuous development is vital to sustaining success. Leadership is no different. Continuous learning involves learning new skills and techniques of leadership. It is also important to stay current on any changes within your industry or professional field.

There are many resources available to facilitate your growth and identify areas of your leadership weakness. Tools such as 360-degree assessments and strength-based questionnaires are a couple of examples. Be open-minded and honest with yourself along your leadership journey.

To continually develop, a leader must practice underdeveloped skills. This deliberate practice focuses on perceived personal weakness. Leveraging SMART goals sets challenges just beyond your comfort level. Celebrate achieving the goal. Ultimately, the goal is to be better than you were yesterday.

Gritty leaders do not wait for opportunity to come knocking. They seek out opportunities that will strengthen their underdeveloped skills.

Stretch opportunities are methods by which you stretch your current skills. You push outside your comfort zone and grow professionally.

You may be thinking, I have so much on my plate now! I don't have capacity! I'm too busy!

Open your mind and be honest with yourself. When you really want something, you will find a way. You will find capacity. Don't let your mind fool you otherwise. Leverage your leadership, delegate, and find capacity for stretch opportunities.

Stretch opportunities are not just busy work of a mundane task. These opportunities leverage your current foundational knowledge and skill set. Stretch opportunities provide a way to take on responsibility above your current level and expand beyond your skills.

Mindfully consider the stretch opportunity. How will it benefit your professional growth? What skills will you develop?

The most meaning stretch opportunities push you into more responsibility to shine as well as provide cross-cultural collaboration within your organization. It provides exposure to show your skills as a leader.

The balance is challenging yourself enough but not

overextending. Ideally, you want 50 to 70 percent chance of success.

Be ready to clearly explain your current skills and why you should get the opportunity. Describe your competencies that make you the best selection.

Consider your approach, plan, and integration into the project. Also, be ready to work hard and demonstrate your commitment. Your grit will lead you though the opportunity.

Stretch opportunities are small trials of your ability to lead. Ensure you have appropriate leadership support before extending yourself to avoid potential floundering.

If a presented stretch opportunity does not meet the level to push your growth, it is important to know how to graciously decline and avoid shooting yourself in the foot for future opportunities.

It is important to determine when it is appropriate to just say no. Here are examples of when to decline stretch opportunities.

- **Opportunities that don't provide the time needed to adequately do your current job.** Keep in mind why you were selected for a specific opportunity. Review each opportunity for risks and benefits. Also, analyze the ability or availability to continue your current tasks. Do not allow your current responsibilities to take a back seat to the newfound opportunity.

- **Opportunities that don't build your strengths.** Stretch opportunities are a venue of growth and professional development. The opportunity should be part of your developmental action plan. Ideally, you should be able to develop a new skill, leadership, or a professional strength. If the presented opportunity doesn't lend to the growth, consider a modification to include growth potential.

- **Opportunities that don't expand your network.** Seek opportunities that provide an avenue for interactions with leaders, potential mentors, and strategic associates. This will provide a new light to showcase your talents. Also, it provides individuals a glimpse at the diversity of your skills.

- **Opportunities that don't develop the reputation you desire.** Consider your personal brand. Does the stretch opportunity align? Aligning the opportunity to your personal brand will ensure you showcase your talents and accomplishments.

If you do turn down an opportunity, do so graciously. Thank the individual who has provided the opportunity. Say that you cannot divide your attention from your currently full schedule. Also, recommend another highly qualified individual for the stretch opportunity.

There is a delicate process of turning down stretch opportunities. Turning down too many will lead others to believe you aren't interested in growth opportunities. Keep this in the back of your mind and provides a solid reason for declining an opportunity.

WARNING: Career suicide can occur when a stretch opportunity is turned down from a senior leader.

Assess the opportunity and the individual proposing the opportunity before turning a stretch opportunity down. The assignment could be a test for another opportunity.

Gritty leaders challenge themselves through calculated risks. They are comfortable being uncomfortable. They frequently step out of their comfort zones to seek opportunities of professional growth and development. Your ability to tolerate awkwardness leads to your ability to project total awesomeness.

Many practice leadership in a box. They stay within some imaginary lines they've built. What's beyond those lines? In the fields of awkwardness, you will find strength, respect, admiration, personal gratification, growth, and enhanced ability to lead others.

Although all leaders want to succeed, part of being a great leader is taking risks and being willing to fail. Attempting failure as well as success is important.

Commitment to yourself will provide the mental security that you have the skills needed.

Leadership is a self-guided journey that requires continuous learning and professional growth. Continuous improvement is striving to improve the status quo and impacts all areas of leadership. Every day in your role, you strive to improve the experience for your team, your customers or patients, your coworkers, your products, and your service.

Make the commitment that will change your life by commitment to personal development. Pushing out of your comfort zone is one of the venues for personal growth. Get comfortable being uncomfortable. Set yourself up for success when you are stretched into uncomfortable situations by setting goals and making them smart. Stretch opportunities are a way of cultivating new skills. Recognize opportunities that will develop new skills versus those that are simply busy work. Leadership is a self-guided journey of professional growth.

BITE OF GRIT

Grit begins with understanding the value of commitment through committing to yourself for personal development.

Results of quick wins and instant results are often short lived.

Inspire to create huge, hairy, audacious goals and cut them in half to create small victories along the way.

To continually develop as a leader, you must practice underdeveloped skills through leveraging your leadership, delegation, and finding capacity for stretch opportunities.

⬛▶ STEP 8 EXERCISE:

Strengthen your grit with Exercise 8 in the GRIT Bootcamp Workbook!

Step 9:

Crush It with Small Wins

Step 9: Crush It with Small Wins

Celebrate your success. Find some humor in your failures.

Sam Walton

Small wins drive perseverance and solidify commitment over time. Recognizing past achievements will stimulate your brain with happy chemicals. Remembering how far you have come will keep you going during tougher times.

Celebrate and recognize your achievements daily. Celebrating develops and builds your muscle of mental strength. Daily recognition is a reminder of the progress you are making on difficult days and show the success you have achieved.

Step 9 is to crush it with small wins.

Everyone has achievements. Don't sell yourself short. Now, what have you done to recognize achievements?

Take a moment and list your achievements. Regardless of the impact of the achievement, if it moved you toward your goal, recognize it. Get out your pen and paper. Better yet, pull out your GRIT workbook. Write down your achievements and make it real.

Do the same for your team. Without your leadership, your team would not have achievements. List the team's achievements also.

As leaders, you are compensated for the performance of our team—good or bad. If the team fails, we fail. You must take responsibility for yourself and the actions and performance of the team.

In leading a team, leaders will relinquish the just-one-of-the-team position and rise to the leader position by setting direction and expectations for the group. This is shown by their separation from the team. You no longer go on lunches or friendly ventures outside of work. You rise to manage the problems and remove barriers. Leaders manage everyone with equality and integrity.

As you lead by example for accepting responsibility and accountability, you will see a change in the culture of your team. Your team members take ownership for outcomes. They also accept responsibility for their own actions and the job they perform. Collaboration is embraced, and the team functions on a higher level.

~~~~~

Acknowledging small wins will create a mindset of success and provide confidence in your mental strength.

Let's develop our accomplishment list through three simple steps:

Step 1: Accomplishments and Achievements

Consider all the accomplishments and achievements you have done throughout your life. Regardless of how small they are, list the accomplishments. One of my accomplishments was getting into PA school. One of my achievements was obtaining my PA license to practice medicine. Another accomplishment was writing my first leadership book. What are your accomplishments?

Step 2: Skills

What skills do you possess? What are your strengths? Consider the skills that helped you achieve the wins. One of my skills or qualities is resilience. As I described previously, I was resilient in my career choice and getting into PA school. I also have a knack for creating analogies. I can relate anything to medicine. For example, elevated blood pressure can be easily related to hydraulic system for a mechanic's understanding. What are your skills?

Step 3: Admire

What do you admire about yourself? Everyone has at least one trait he or she admires. If you only think of the negatives, can you turn the negative into positives? For example, I am quiet in crowds, thus I absorb more conversations and insights while around others. A common Pinterest meme is "I'm not boss; I have leadership skills." Also, "I'm not a perfectionist; I strive for excellence." Turning a negative trait into a positive trait is a secret of mental strength. Identify your trait and ensure it is positive.

Now let's review the list. Does anything stand out to you? How do you feel when you read it? When I completed my list, I felt proud and humbled. I had forgotten several accomplishments. I too have moments of doubt and need to remind myself to build my mental strength. This list is helpful on difficult days.

Who's in your social circle? Consider your influence. If you surround yourself with successful people, you are more likely to be successful. Positivity generates positivity. The individuals who help you grow and develop should be kept closer in your circle.

If you find yourself in a state of negativity, look around. Who is in your circle? Rid yourself of negativity.

~~~~~

Happiness leads to success. Think about it. Have you ever seen a successful *unhappy* person? How could you consider people successful if they are always unhappy? Clearly, there is an imbalance.

Positivity is stimulating. It fuels high performers and allows individuals to lower their emotional shield. Positivity builds people up, which builds self-confidence. The higher self-confidence will build mental strength. Foster and cultivate positivity on your team.

According to happiness expert Shawn Achor, there are five simple steps to cultivate positivity (Achor, 2014).

Sounds pretty simple, huh? You're probably thinking that it is common sense. The funny thing about leadership is sometimes we need a dose of common sense! Individuals get so wrapped up in the daily grind that the fundamentals are missed.

Let's dig deeper into these steps that help achieve wins.

Step 1: Surround Yourself with Positivity

When you look around your office or your team's workspace, what do you notice? Creating a culture of positivity begins with infusing your workspace with the things that make you happy.

In my workspace, I have a small four-by-four selfie of my husband, my girls, and me. I printed it off a black-and-white printer. I hastily taped it to the wall. I smile every time I see the photo. I feel at peace and remember the day the photo was taken. My husband and I were so young in our relationship.

Everyone is unique in what creates feelings of positivity. For me, a paper photo brings happiness. Others may prefer plants, children, artwork, or decorations. Encourage the environment as an influence of positivity.

Step 2: Move It!

Move it! You got it! Just exercise!

Exercise creates positivity through the release of endorphins, the feel-good biochemicals we want to hack.

The release of endorphins reduce stress, reduce anxiety, and increase happiness. It really is a natural high.

Exercise also changes your physical appearance. Changes in appearance as result of exercise is often a confidence booster. As we know, a boost in confidence boosts mental strength.

Step 3: Showcase Your Strengths

Consider a skill you know you have mastered. Immediately, you sit a little taller, hold your head higher, and speak with confidence. Now consider a skill that you consider underdeveloped. Shrink a little? Naturally, we find ourselves limiting the use of the underdeveloped skill. Instead, focus on your greatest strength.

Showcasing strengths is another way of building up individuals and providing a path for them to shine. It provides a venue for the senior individual to mentor someone with an underdeveloped skill. In the long run, you will have a higher-performing team and greater collaboration.

Step 4: Thank You

In the Southern states, we say "please" and "thank you" frequently. We are known for asking permission, and many times we are "fixin' to" do something. Okay, the last one just always makes me giggle. I may be guilty on occasion of this Southern nicety.

In my leadership role, I interact with individuals across the nation. My emails are always courteous and include "please, thank you." My cultural adjustment was understanding that not all regions followed these Southern conventions. Early in my career, I would become defensive and irritated at emails. Once I understood the regional culture of the north and west as more direct, I no longer viewed receiving emails as demanding.

Consider the things you are most thankful for. How about over the past two days? Have you acknowledged your gratitude? The simple act of expressing gratitude will generate positivity.

Step 5: Be Kind

Kindness is contagious. Acts of kindness are positivity in action. Many including me follow the well-known phrase of "do unto others." Whether you are driven by spiritual leading of actions or just karma, kindness is a simple method to show appreciation and respect to others.

There is no way to know what every individual is facing. So many individuals are carrying tons of emotional baggage that often transposes into everyday negative interactions. As a leader, recognize an individual's frustration is beyond you and the position. Lead with kindness and respect.

Crushing it with small wins is creating a culture of positivity in which you celebrate all achievements regardless of size. Maintaining a list of achievements will remind you of how far you have come along your journey.

An achievement list will also build mental strength in times of difficulty. Cultivate an environment for achievements through positivity, exercise, strength, gratitude, and kindness.

BITE OF GRIT

Gritty leaders crush it with small wins through creating a culture of positivity in which individuals celebrate achievements regardless of the size.

Remember to keep a running list of accomplishments, which captures achievements, skills, and positive traits.

Inspire others through positivity, which yields lower emotional shields, higher performance, and self-confidence.

Thank your team and keep in mind that you need your team more than they need you, for without them, you have no one to lead.

STEP 9 EXERCISE:

Strengthen your grit with Exercise 9 in the GRIT Bootcamp Workbook!

Step 10:

Remember to Dwell on the Past

Step 10: Remember to Dwell on the Past

May you have the hindsight to know where you have been, the foresight to know where you are going, and the insight to know when you have gone too far.

Anonymous

The majority of leaders at some point in their leadership have questioned a decision that was made. Every effective leader reserves time to reflect on the past.

Leveraging foresight, leaders guide their current decisions through learning from the past, mindfulness of the present, and understanding the potential consequences of the future. Through the diversity of the team you create, you surround yourselves with individuals who offer different perspectives of a situation. They provide a fresh view into your everyday decisions. Foresight provides a venue for making intuitive and educated decisions.

Step 10 is remembering to dwell on the past.

Have you ever heard the wise saying "If I knew then what I know now, things would have been different"? That is reflection and the essence of foresight. Taking time to reflect upon decisions made and outcomes will facilitate your professional growth.

Gritty leaders leverage past experiences to guide future decisions. They analyze previous outcomes to ensure they are making the best decisions possible.

There are several ways you can learn from past experiences and strengthen foresight:

1. **Lead with diversity.** This relates back to self-awareness. When you surround yourselves with diverse individuals, you develop a better-rounded team. By only surrounding ourselves with like-minded individuals, your teams will have your strengths and our weaknesses. This is also known as similarity bias.

2. **Active mindful listening.** Listening is a critical skill that anyone should have, especially a leader. Listen to the full discussion before formulating a response. Are you hearing similar concerns from several team members? If so, by foresight, you could determine an emerging trend or future consequence.

3. **Read widely**. Develop an industry understanding. You are not expected to be subject matter expert in your field. However, you are expected to have a general understanding of the industry. This is vital

to understanding how to best lead within the industry.

4. **Systematic approach**. Think systematically. Consider the situation and leverage your foresight to determine the consequence of decisions. If successful, you have a repeatable systemic approach to similar situations.

5. **Predictions**. Over time, you will notice similar outcomes based upon your systemic approach. The outcomes become almost predictable. Practice making predictions alone as well as with your team. Test the predictions against reality. Are you identifying trends?

Dwelling on the past will ensure you are taking responsibility and accountability. The leader's role is to be accountable to the members of the team through leading by example and removing barriers. Accountability is accepting the outcomes of an initiative, good or bad.

Our job as leaders is to remove barriers and roadblocks to secure the team's success. The team's success is our measuring stick. Consider the obstacles that are creating difficulty for the team. Identify solutions for the obstacles and how to remove them.

You may discover that you haven't upheld a standard for the team, perhaps through accountability or consistency. If the team is far from meeting the target, take a look in the mirror.

Are there inconsistencies in the example you are setting?

To lead by example, we must be responsible for our actions. We must set the example for others to follow. Then we must follow the same rules, policies, and regulations we have required of the team.

For example, the supervisor cannot like a post on social media and manage a team member's performance for the same activity. Also, on the implementation of a strict travel provision, the leader cannot stay at the swankiest hotel in the city or initiate strict spending and purchase a luxury car.

Do any leaders immediately come to your mind? How does it make you feel? Aggravated? Angry? Frustrated?

If that statement stings, take a look in the mirror, think about your actions, and make changes.

Guess what? Your team feels the same way when you don't lead by example.

Think before you act. All of our actions can impact our team. *Keep in mind that you are on stage and your team is watching.* The higher your position, the bigger your stage.

Think of your team as having a savings account. All of the trust, active listening, relationship building, etc. are small deposits into an account. Over time, you have a solid partnership and a nice nest egg with your team.

Each time you fail to lead by example causes a withdrawal from the account. The amount of the withdrawal is determined by the actions of the leader. Betrayal or perceived betrayal will result in large withdrawals leaving nothing in the account.

It is an honor for a team to instill their trust in you to lead them. This privilege is not to be taken lightly. We are obligated to covet that trust by setting the best example and always having the team's best interest in mind.

Leading by example can easily be applied to your leadership in several ways:

- Be willing to do anything you would ask of others.

- Follow the rules as closely as you expect your team members to follow.

- Be cautious not to interrupt any team member, especially if you are critical of someone else interrupting.

Take a moment and think about your leadership style, your values, and your actions. Consider if you need to make any adjustments.

Placing blame is often seen in leadership positions. When things go south, individuals are ready to point fingers and isolate the individual or thing that caused the issue. This is the easy route. It's much easier to point out someone and place blame. Mentally strong leaders accept the blame and create action plans.

Recognize that placing blame is a detriment to everyone including the leadership you are attempting to establish. The blamed individual will feel betrayed by you, which will impact the trust you are developing as we will later learn. If we blame the process, the individual who created the process will feel betrayed.

Stepping up and accepting responsibility can be viewed as an advantage. It is an opportunity for us to showcase our skills and abilities. If we accept blame, we then have a chance to show how we can manage in the face of adversity or through a crisis. This will advance your team, your initiatives, and your leadership reputation.

Remember to dwell on the past to learn from previous decisions. Understand the downstream effects of past decisions, be mindful of present decisions, and analyze consequences of future decisions. A mentally strong leaders sets an example and hold themselves to the same standards as the rest of the team. Strong leaders accept responsibility for all actions, positive or negative. Mentally strong leaders accept responsibility and reflect upon outcomes to strengthen decision-making skills.

BITE OF GRIT

Gritty leaders leverage past experience through reflect to guide future decisions.

Repeatable, systemic approaches to situations will yield consistency in leadership through predictable, consistent outcomes.

Inspire through leading by example by being willing to do what is asked of others, following the same rules, and listening actively without interruption.

Take responsibility and accountability for bad outcomes too, as gritty leaders accept the balance and manage through adversity.

STEP 10 EXERCISE:

Strengthen your grit with Exercise 10 in the GRIT Bootcamp Workbook!

Step 11:

Know Your Superpower

Step 11: Know Your Superpower

A leader takes people where they want to go. A great leader takes people where they did not necessarily want to go, but ought to be.

Rosalyn Carter

Successful leaders are mentally strong. We are just mentally wired that way. Notice I've included you? It takes mental strength to know when we need to focus on our own development.

This leads to the question: is mental strength proportional to the level of success of the leader?

Possibly.

There is evidence to support the higher-level positions are seated by mentally strong individuals. High-level leaders are often faced with the bigger risks and decisions. Mentally strong leaders often have the following traits:

- Self-belief

- Desire or motivation
- Ability to manage anxiety or stress
- Focus
- Work–life balance
- Visionary outlook

Step 11 is about knowing your superpower or strength you bring forward.

Gritty leaders know their strengths and weaknesses. They excel in leveraging their personal strengths. Also, they identify others to compensate for their weakness.

Compensating for weakness begins with surround yourself with experts. If you are the smartest and most skilled of your team, you need new team members. As a leader, your job is to identify and lead experts—not be the expert. Otherwise, you are surrounded by individuals who will flounder in crisis and share your weaknesses. By knowing your weaknesses, you will also know your strengths. As a leader, you showcase other's strengths.

Today's leadership focuses on strength-based leading. Strength-based leadership is founded in leaders knowing their strongest contributions to the team. Weaker or underdeveloped skills are supplemented by others.

Strength-based leadership is a blending of four areas: execution, influence, strategy, and relationship building, of which many leaders will have an overlap and blending.

Execution is the skill of getting things done. It is the ability to take a project and bring it to completion. Execution sounds fairly easy. Rest assured, the execution skill is a strength. This strength is seen in people who can easily control tasks and manage people to get the job done. It is a position of direct and indirect influence. Executional strong leaders are highly focused on outcomes.

Influence is the strength to persuade or influence others to perform a task and support an initiative or idea. It is the skill of selling or persuading others to your idea or situational position. Influence can be achieved through position of authority. However, it is most effective through leadership influence. The influence leads to individuals completing a desired outcome because they accomplish it, not because it is required. Influence-driven leaders are cool under pressure and persuasive.

Strategy is the strength of assimilating information into the big picture. It is the skill of seeing beyond the day-to-day operations and into the larger vision. Strategic leaders remind the team of how their daily activities drive the overall mission. Strategic-driven leaders embody the team with the sense of purpose through daily activities.

Relationship building is the strength of connecting with team members and moving them toward a common goal. Relationship building focuses on initiating and maintaining partnerships that are mutually beneficial to both parties. Relationships are the keys to getting things done. Emotional connections within the relationships lend to a stronger empathy toward an individual. You will have a better understanding of the individual's motivational drivers. Through the connections, you encourage others and leverage emotional intelligence to strengthen the team.

Relationship building is critical to your success as a leader. Without the skills to develop relationships, you are guaranteed to stall on your career track. Servant-leaders naturally have the soft skills of relationship building.

Think back to building resilience within the team. Building resilience begins with building trust. Whom do people trust? The majority of people don't blindly trust a stranger. Trust develops over time through relationships.

If you struggle with relationships or had a few go sour, here are some tips to relationship building:

1. People skills: strengthen communication, problem-solving, conflict resolution, and active listening.

2. Relationship needs: define the needs of each individual in the relationship.

3. Schedule time: to build a relationship, you must make time for it.

4. Emotional intelligence: develop your skill of understanding other's emotions.

5. Avoid gossip: Gossiping about coworkers will damage relationships. Instead, seek them out and resolve the conflict.

You may be thinking that many of these tips are just common sense. Well, they are! Sometimes it's good to be reminded.

Having good relationships is a big advantage to strength-based leadership and easily lends to showcasing the best of your team. You and the team are superstars every day.

To showcase, you must learn to delegate. Gritty leaders leverage other's expertise and delegate tasks to the appropriate skill sets. Delegation is not a way of discrediting the value you bring to the team. Delegation is a way to showcase that you leverage your resources effectively.

Focusing on an individual's strength will automatically generate more engagement and joy from the team. The team members are focused within their comfort zone and greatest knowledge. They have pride in their work and demonstrate the value they bring to the team. As a result, you generate superior outcomes.

Strength-based leadership also enhances the overall performance of the team. By knowing the team's strength, you also know the weakness. This provides an advantage during the hiring process to ensure gaps within the team's knowledge are addressed. The team is more well-rounded and deliver better outcomes.

Strength-based leadership is a balance. You must be mindful of the ambitions of the team and not typecast them into their role. Morale can easily turn sour if someone feels they are passed over for a promotional opportunity due to typecasting.

Ensure you have a backup plan for the team member.

While one member may be the expert, ensure that other team members have some knowledge of subject. Don't rest the fate of the team on the shoulders of one. It is self-destructive for one team member to hold all the knowledge. Gritty leaders have contingency plans to ensure the project is supported in an absence of a team member.

We have reviewed many aspects of strength-based leadership. I'm confident that you are recognizing the strengths you bring. If you are stuck, let's explore how you determine your superpower.

Isolate yourself. Self-reflection starts with alone time. Solitude provides a venue for self-reflection and insights. It is acquired by being free from the input of others and technology. Solitude also strengthens empathy, drives creativity, and personal insights to discover your superstrengths.

Strengthen empathy. Alone time separates you from your inner circle and provides time to reflect upon how you interact with different individuals. You begin to develop a deeper compassion for others and strengthen your emotional intelligence.

Drive productivity and creativity. Most individuals are distracted by being in a group of people. They long for their designated work location that provides them privacy to collect their thoughts and complete tasks. Also, being alone provides your mind the ability to wander, thus lending to the creative side.

Personal insights. Alone time provides a venue to become lost in your thoughts. You begin to become more comfortable in your leadership and have a deeper understanding of the decisions made. Also, you can reflect upon your personal brand and determine if you are on the most appropriate track for your personal development.

Gritty leaders rely on compromise to execute strength-based leadership. You compromise with leadership, clients, and your team. Perhaps your initial proposal isn't feasible when discussing with the experts of your team. You compromise and modify the proposal, yet still achieving the overall goal. While compromise is a necessary strength, overcompromise can lead to a downward spiral of people pleasing.

People Pleaser

At some point in leadership, everyone is a people pleaser. Consider the last time you received criticism or constructive feedback. What did you do? Did you make modifications to meet the standard or fulfill any deficits? Of course you did! This is people pleasing. In any leadership, people pleasing is appropriate at certain levels or with certain requests.

While people pleasing has a negative concentration, there are positive aspects of people pleasing. As a servant-leader, you tend to value people, serve selflessly, and have high levels of emotional intelligence. You tend to value talents, deliver an inspirational approach, and are great people advocates. Your team feels a higher sense of value. Overall, your team is more loyal to you and engaged. You demonstrate a greater ability to lead by direct and indirect influence, thus achieving greater results more efficiently.

It's not appropriate to support all requests at all times. People pleasing is a balance. Overpleasing can be detrimental. Similarly, there are negative characteristics of people pleasing. These leaders have difficulty with delegation, avoid taking charge, tolerate poor performers, sugarcoat responses, and can become resentful of team members. People pleasing can impact your leadership by impairing your ability to reach your full potential through continuously falling short of stated expectations.

How do you know when people pleasing is toxic or detrimental to your leadership?

Many times, the people-pleasing cycle is through extreme compromise. For example, you decide the business should be open on the weekend. The staff or coworkers give pushback. As a modern-day leader, you look for compromise. One compromise leads to another. The next thing you know, the result is far from the initial objective. The result is a culture of entitlement with little resilience. The team is not mentally strong. Another example would be the request to work 36 hours and be paid for a 40-hour work week or for one staff member to consistently leave one hour early, while the rest of the team pick up the slack on the end-of-shift duties. Consider the resentment building among the team.

If you end up in this endless cycle of people pleasing, be aware. Besides the obvious, there are several ways it is detrimental to your leadership (Nieuwhof, 2017).

Lose sight of the mission. The cycle of people pleasing will lead to scarifying the mission of the organization you lead. The extensive compromise leads to the team members going in different directions. This misdirection leads to individualized agendas and loss of the overall focus of the team.

Lose self-respect and credibility. Continuous people pleasing leads to the feeling of selling out. The constant, extensive compromise leads to feeling internal disappointment in your leadership style. As a result, you lose credibility in the team. Restore credibility by letting individuals know if they're not meeting the standards. Don't continue to encourage them that they are doing well. You may win the battle but will lose the war.

Lose high performers. The cycle of people pleasing will result in discontent among the higher-performing members. They grow resentful of the lack of direction, increase of subpar coworkers, low accountability, and inefficiency. These characteristics leads to an undesirable work environment. The high-performing team members will just slowly phase out of the team without uproar. Ensure you have a stimulating environment for the high performers.

No one is truly happy. Losing the high performers leaves you with a team of mid to low performers. You potentially sacrificed the mission by overcompromising. Over time, your team will become less loyal, as they feel you are becoming more of a "yes" person. At the end of the day, no one on the team is happy.

How do you know if you are a people pleaser?

Self-awareness will provide insights to your potential people-pleasing tendencies. Reflect upon these five simple questions:

- Is it difficult to say "no" to people?
- Do you struggle to meet everyone's needs and at times forego your own needs?
- Upon feeling rejected, do you criticize yourself?
- How do you feel when conflict arises? Nervous or anxious?
- Does positive feedback provide you self-assurance?

How do you avoid the people-pleasing trap?

Generally, the people-pleasing cycle is triggered during a state of change. Implementing change management principles and involving the team in the change will help avert the endless cycle.

Know your superpower and your strength. Mentally strong leaders know and leverage their strengths, which are generally rooted in strategy, execution, influence, and relationship building.

One of the best resources on discovering your strengths is *Strength-Based Leadership* by Tom Rath and Barry Conchie. With a quick assessment, you will discover how to best leverage your strengths and your team's strengths.

Leverage the strengths of your team members to create a high-functioning team. Know your team members and keep a pulse on morale. Compromise where appropriate but do not fall into a vicious trap of people pleasing. Only you can determine the best actions and next steps in your leadership journey.

BITE OF GRIT

Gritty leaders have awareness of personal strength showcasing the team's strengths and surround themselves with experts in their weaknesses.

Relationship building focuses on initiating mutually beneficial partnerships as the key to getting things done.

Isolate yourself for self-reaction to identify your superpower.

Toxic environment is created through excessive people pleasing and overcompromising by the leader.

STEP 11 EXERCISE:

Strengthen your grit with Exercise 11 in the GRIT Bootcamp Workbook!

Step 12:

You Gotta Have GRIT

Step 12: You Gotta Have GRIT

It is not the strongest of the species that survive, nor the most intelligent, but the ones most responsive to change.

Charles Darwin

Do you often feel that some leaders are lucky? That things just magically happen for others? Their stars are always aligned and always receiving cosmic blessings. Rest assured, this is rarely the case.

If you asked successful leaders such as Bill Gates from Microsoft and Jeff Bezos from Amazon about how they achieved success, they would respond with grit and perseverance.

Grit has nothing to do with talent. You can be the most talented individual in your field or sport, but it will not guarantee you will always succeed.

Grit is not related to intelligence. It is not determined

by your score on an IQ test. It is also unrelated to your number or types of degrees.

Step 12 is this: You gotta have grit. Along with grit is the drive of passion.

Passion is the internal drive that leads you along your journey. Perseverance is the loyalty felt for your passion. It is your commitment. Grit leverages the steadfast pursuit of perseverance in overcoming obstacles to achieve goals over an extended time. The passion makes the venture feel less like work and more of a journey.

As seen throughout the years, grit is a better predictor of success than talent. Grit reflects an individual's long-term commitment to goals.

Grit is influenced through mindset. Mindset is your mental attitude. It is your mental assessment of situations and challenges.

Psychologist Carol Dweck (2007) defines mindset as the way an individual approaches life. Mindset is an attitude toward tasks. Mindset determines who will succeed or fail.

Mindset is a huge contributor into the development of grit. Some believe they are at their physical or mental threshold, while others believe their talent is enough for success and does not need to be cultivated. The way an individual views these components determines the mindset. One's mindset is growth or fixed.

Individuals with a fixed mindset have difficulty thinking outside the box. They believe their strengths and limitations are predetermined. This predetermined, fixed mindset will subconsciously hold you back. You believe in the limitations and have difficulty overcoming the mental restrictions in times of stress, thus stalling in times of difficulty or faced with challenge. A fixed mindset creates self-limitation.

Some may believe they simply do not have the skills or intelligence. Fixed mindsets feel they do not have the capability to improve. They tend to give up when faced with adversity. Fixed mindsets tend to have pessimistic outlooks.

We all know individuals of a fixed mentality. However, that individual is not you. You are showing your growth mindset by reading this book and developing grit.

Gritty leaders have a growth mindset. They believe their abilities are flexible and continue to develop. They are flexible and innovative. Gritty leaders are less frustrated when things don't go as planned.

Leaders with a growth mindset believe they can continue to evolve and improve. They are optimistic and proactively look for solutions.

Surround yourself with growth-minded individuals. Create a culture of growth. As a servant-leader, this will come naturally. Gritty leaders cultivate grittier individuals. Overall, the team becomes stronger and self-leading.

Leverage your newfound mental strength to cultivate your leadership excellence. Let's dive into the twelve ways to achieve leadership excellence as defined by Benedict Chidile.

1. **Be original**

   Develop your brand. Know your values and what you represent. Be consistent with your leadership style, moods, and decisions. Consistency will strengthen your brand.

2. **Support a struggling colleague**

   Supporting others is a way of showcasing your emotional intelligence. You have the skills to identify a struggle as well as mentor the individuals in the challenge.

3. **Be an effective team player**

   Collaboration is key for any leader. As a leader, you will work with a diverse array of individual personalities. Effective team members are high contributors. Also, they will need to understand how to bring out the best in challenging personalities as an effective team member.

4. **Think results-oriented in tasks**

   You will be expected to deliver results. As you create processes and initiatives, consider your measures of success. How will you show value in the initiatives? What are your metrics?

5. **Avoid envy and jealousy**

   Envy and jealousy can be the downfall of a leader. It is toxic. It destroys relationships and pulls your focus from the mission. Turn envy into celebration. You will be viewed as more collaborative. Nurture your partnership with others.

6. Appreciate other's efforts

If someone contributes to the team or project, recognize the efforts. Everyone wants to feel appreciated for hard work. Lack of acknowledgement and appreciation of the team is demoralizing and can destroy a high-performing team.

7. Think outside the box

Develop a growth mindset. Mentally strong leaders have a growth mindset. They are open to suggestions and frequently thinking of how to improve processes. These leaders embrace change and development.

8. Strive to fail

Nothing is learned in victory. Growth is achieved through pushing outside your comfort zone and failing. Through failure, you can showcase your leadership skills of action-plan development and execution.

9. Focus on the objective

In the daily grind, it is easy to lose focus on the big picture. Reflect daily on the initiatives and objectives of the day. Do they align with the mission or bigger picture? If not, what adjustments can be made to ensure they do? Determine the most appropriate initiative to focus your energy. Trying to focus on too many initiatives will spread you too thin and impact your results.

10. **Strive for win-win with others**

   When one team member wins, the entire team wins. You also win as the leader of the team. Set individuals up for success. Identify their strengths, provide opportunities, and guide them to success.

11. **Be proactive**

   Seek out opportunities and do not wait for them to be handed to you. Being proactive will show your initiative and go-getter attitude. It demonstrates your willingness to accept a challenge and be a change agent.

12. **Flexible to change**

   Leaders must be flexible. Initiatives change, missions change, and senior leadership change. You must develop the skills to change midstream when the situation warrants change. Adjust to change will showcase your flexibility.

Leadership excellence is shown through the committed development of the team. This does not happen overnight. Leadership excellence is developed over time on the foundation of the leader's values and growth mindset.

BITE OF GRIT

Grit is the steadfast pursuit of perseverance in overcoming obstacles to achieve goals over an extended time.

Restrictive or fixed mindsets tend to give up when faced with adversity due to inflexible beliefs in self-limitation.

Instill within your team a culture of growth, which will lead to wins for the team by showcasing individual strengths.

Thrive with leadership excellence by being there with your values and consistency with your brand.

STEP 12 EXERCISE:

Strengthen your grit with Exercise 12 in the GRIT Bootcamp Workbook!

What's Next?

What's Next?

Leadership is a journey. Each one
of us has to take our own path,
and their our own way.

David Gergen

Throughout this book, you have discovered the twelve steps to develop mental strength. The next step is up to you. If you have completed the workbook along your journey, you are stronger today than when you started. Every day, the goal is to be stronger than yesterday.

Developing grit begins with knowing yourself. Discovering happiness, growth, and success is the first step. Consider your daily activities. Do the activities bring you true joy and happiness? If you aren't doing what you love, then your mind will not deem you successful. Your mental strength will diminish. The fancy car and lavish home will not provide you the heartfelt success that you long for.

Your life purpose should make you emotional. It should bring warmth to your chest and a sense of inner peace. Your life purpose can change over time, but the foundation will not.

You are you. You are unique. You are the only one with your leadership style. Your approach is uniquely your own. And your mental strength is determined by you in a journey you define.

Embrace the journey of achieving your goal. No one is perfect at the first attempt. It's like riding a bike or walking. The mentally strong learn from mistakes and embrace the process.

Servant leadership embodies the essence of GRIT. Being gritty is the ability to continue moving forward in the face of failure. Being gritty is continuing to challenge yourself in professional development. Being gritty is having and achieving purposeful SMART goals. Being gritty is continuing to strive toward and knowing your purpose.

Transition from reactive to proactive. Don't wait for opportunity. Seek it out.

You are ready. You are empowered. Let's put your grit to the test as you have already done. Discover your passion and perseverance to knock out your goals.

And always have GRIT for breakfast.

Enjoy the journey!

Cara

P.S. I would love to know how you have focused your GRIT to achieve success. Send me an email at carabramlett@yahoo.com. I cannot wait to hear from you !

Thank you for purchasing this book!

I hope the book has provided you insights into your leadership style and management. Each one of us are different and unique in our approach to leadership.

Never give up and know you are strong. Lead with your servant heart and be guided by your moral compass.

Reviews are *critical* to the survival of any indie author like me! If you have benefited from this book or feel someone else would, please take a few moments and rate this book!

Sharing is caring!

MORE FREE STUFF!

Are you interested in *free* leadership books? Sign up to be on the launch team!

You get an advance *free* reviewer copy of my next book. You would need to read the book within a week, provide feedback, and leave a review on go-live day! ☺

It's that *easy*! To join, click here➔ PICK ME!

I would love to hear from you! Share your journey or challenge you are experiencing. Email me at carabramlett@yahoo.com.

Enjoy the journey!

Cara Bramlett

P.S. Don't forget your bonus!

Download the Manager's Toolbox HERE!

References

(2018, 01). Retrieved from Mind Tools: https://www.mindtools.com/pages/article/albrecht-stress.htm

(2018, February). Retrieved from Mind Tools: https://www.mindtools.com/pages/article/newTCS_95.htm

Achor, S. (2014, March). Retrieved from Wharton @ Work:
https://executiveeducation.wharton.upenn.edu/thought-leadership/wharton-at-work/2014/03/positivity-habits

Crum, A., & Crum, T. (2015, 09 03). *Harvard Business Review*. Retrieved from https://hbr.org/2015/09/stress-can-be-a-good-thing-if-you-know-how-to-use-it

Dweck, C. (2007). *Mindset*.

Estacio, PhD, E. (2018). The Imposter Syndrome Remedy.

Klein, PhD, K., & Bowman, E. H. (2013, October). *https://executiveeducation.wharton.upenn.edu/*. Retrieved from Wharton @ Work:
https://executiveeducation.wharton.upenn.edu/thought-leadership/wharton-at-work/2013/10/building-resilience

Nieuwhof, C. (2017). *5 Ways People Pleasing Undermines Your Leadership*. Retrieved from Carey Nieuwhof:

https://careynieuwhof.com/5-ways-people-pleasing-undermines-your-leadership/

LEADING WITH THE CLINICAL MIND:

Connecting Management to Medicine

Imagine leading your high-functioning team to meet the organization's goals as an industry leader. You are followed for who you are and what you represent. Your team members willingly share adversity and pending threats. Make this a reality through understanding leadership techniques through our clinical mindset. Learn how to relate to each member of your team and know how to maximize each one's unique skills. Learn how to leverage skills of communication, coaching, conflict resolution, and much more!

As clinical professionals, you have naturally dedicated your life to serving patients. Understanding how to relate leadership to medicine makes the transition smooth for clinically minded individuals.

Any clinical professional can be an effective leader! This book will teach you management concepts through medical analogies.

You will also discover the following:

- Ten techniques to combat feeling *overwhelmed*
- Activities to develop emotional intelligence
- The most successful method of employee engagement
- How to *speak* so others love to *listen*

- Steps to a call-to-action plan
- Tips for managing high-volume emails
- And much more!

Get the book!

Do you wonder how some managers lead rock star teams and rise above expectations?

Are you tired of struggling with leading individuals you don't directly manage? Are you ready to take people with you and have others follow your lead?

Are you ready to take charge of your leadership? New to management or looking for a quick refresher?

Imagine leading individuals through inspiration instead of just by being the boss. Your team is inspired to come to work every day. You and your team feel valued at the end of every day. You lead the rock star team and rise above expectations. You have a devoted team of followers who follow you.

Is this your world? Sound like a dream world?

Learn the power of servant leadership mastery!

- The number one way to get people to follow you

- Discover the four-step method to solve any problem and be an effective decision maker
- And so much more!

Bonuses: Manager's Toolbox Templates and a mini book, *Mental Toughness for the Servant-Leader: How to Avoid Bad Decisions through Controlling Emotions*

If you are tired of long books that leave you still searching for answers, are you ready for fluff-free nuts-and-bolts lessons? Ready to learn or develop your soft skills? Then this book is one you *cannot* afford to miss!

Servant Leadership Roadmap is creating powerful effective leaders one individual at a time!

About the Author

Cara Bramlett, PA-C, is a clinical program director for a large health care organization. She continues to practice weekly in a primary care setting. Cara is passionate about ensuring each leader recognizes his or her dream of achieving leadership.

Through the promotion of self-improvement and professional development, Cara inspires and motivates others to deliver excellence in patient care and leadership leveraging integrity, honesty, collaboration, and empathy. Cara supports individuals and organizations through strong technical skills, problem solving, innovation, and unique clinical strategic perspective vested in evidence-based clinical practice.

Cara enjoys spending time with her five kids and two grandkids. She also enjoys spending time with her husband, riding motorcycles, and playing golf.

SERVANT LEADERSHIP BOOTCAMP

Learn more at servantleaderjourney.com, follow me on Facebook, or connect with me on LinkedIn!

48990452R00105

Made in the USA
Lexington, KY
19 August 2019